LETTERS FROM YEMEN
By
Mary Lou Currier

Mary Lou Currier

ISBN-13:978-1500311711
ISBN-10:1500311715

Dedicated to Mom, Dad, and Mrs. A.

In appreciation to Evelyn Bell and Jenine Hemphill who encouraged me to publish the Letters from Yemen, and to Evelyn for her hours spent proof reading the letters. Also in appreciation to my niece Meagan Reed who advised me and prepared the Letters for publication.

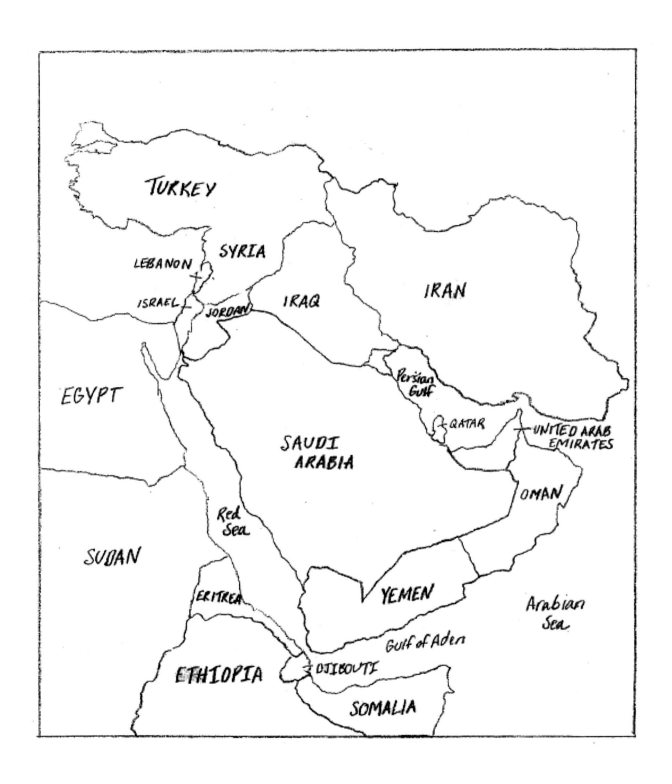

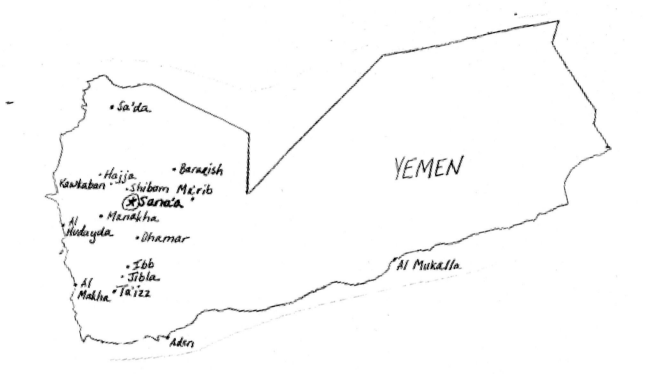

Preface

I was a Peace Corps Volunteer in the Republic of Yemen from November, 1991, through January, 1994. The letters that follow are the letters I wrote home to my family and friends, describing my life in Yemen as a TEFL (teaching English as a foreign language) teacher at the University of Sana'a in the capital, Sana'a. Peace Corps, created during President Kennedy's administration, has sent volunteers all over the Developing World for the past fifty years. The volunteers have served as teachers, nurses, midwives, and health care trainers. Volunteers have also assisted people in their host countries to improve their agriculture practices and establish small businesses, among other assistance programs.

Volunteers make a two year commitment to serve in the Peace Corps after an intensive three-month training in the host country that consists of cross cultural awareness, health issues, and the language spoken in the host country. Countries request the US to send volunteers. The US pays the volunteers a subsistence monthly salary, comparable to, in my case, what Yemeni teachers earned. They are supposed to live simply, not in compounds as many in the diplomatic corps do, and to use the local transportation. Often, volunteers who serve in villages do so without electricity and running water. I was fortunate because I lived in Sana'a and had both electricity and running water.

Peace Corps Volunteers are expected to refrain from expressing their personal political views or their opinions about local politics and customs and are not permitted to promote religious beliefs. They are expected to refrain from reporting to CIA personnel or members of other spy organizations information they may have gained, based on personal experiences. In other words, Peace Corps Volunteers, although they represent the United States, are in their host countries to help, to learn and to bring this knowledge back to the USA to share with Americans so they can better understand the cultures of the World.

Yemen is located on the Arabian Peninsula, south of Saudi Arabia, bordered by Oman, the Red Sea, and the Arabian Sea. Although it has a proud, ancient culture, was a main route for camel caravans transporting incense north, it is one of the poorest countries in the World, just relatively recently emerging from the Middle Ages. It is a conservative Islamic country; the practice of other religions is forbidden without special permission from the government, and the official language is Arabic.

There were two separate Yemens, South Yemen and North Yemen, until the two countries united in 1990. This has not been an easy union. South Yemen was occupied by the British until the mid-1960's when unrest finally drove the British from South Yemen. The British did little to develop South Yemen or to improve the lives of the citizens in the 100 years they occupied the country. Among the groups fighting against British occupation was a Marxist group which has had a great deal of influence into the present time. North Yemen was invaded by Turkey but was never completely conquered because the mountainous country and fortified villages built on mountain tops made such villages impenetrable. Turkey spread a conservative brand of Islam and cultural customs followed today, long after the fall of the Ottoman Empire. The British and the Ottomans drew a line between the two areas of their influence. This line eventually became the border between North and South Yemen.

North Yemen was ruled by Imams who kept the people poor and uneducated as a means of control. The country was isolated from the rest of the World until the early 1960's. After the death of Imam Ahmed in 1962, civil war erupted between the Republicans, supported by Egypt and the Soviet Union, and the Royalists who supported Imam Ahmad's son Muhammad al-Badir. Saudi Arabia and Britain supported Muhammad al-Badir. The Republicans, led by Colonel Abdullah Salah who became president and remained so until 2012, eventually won even though fierce fighting between tribes continued for some time, and tribal conflicts still flare up. South Yemen became the country of the People's Democratic Republic of Yemen (PDRY). North Yemen became known as the Yemen Arabic Republic (YAR). Eventually, after decades of discussion and disagreement, the two countries united and became The Republic of Yemen in 1990.

Since the unification there has been an uneasy alliance between the two former countries. By agreement, the president of the Republic of Yemen was from the North and the vice-president was from the South. The threat of civil war existed during the time I lived in Yemen and finally erupted in the spring of 1994, three months after I left the country. The south supported secession from the union and failed to win. Although the civil war was short lived, there is still an uneasy relationship between the central government in Sana'a and many of the tribes, compounded by the recent uprising as part of the Arab Spring and the growing influence of Al-Qaeda, especially in the south.

The Peace Corps was an active organization in Yemen for a couple of decades before the Gulf War occurred. At the start of the war, Peace Corps pulled the volunteers out of the country as a precaution for the volunteers' safety. Although Yemen did not officially participate in the war, they were sympathetic towards Iraq. Iraq had historically been sympathetic to Yemen's problems with Saudi Arabia, and many Yemenis liked Saddam Hussein because they saw him as an Arabic hero who stood up for all Arabs against Western colonialism. This support angered the United States and its allies. Saudi Arabia deported thousands of Yemeni workers because of Yemen's support of Iraq, and countries such as Kuwait discontinued financial support. The removal of this help proved disastrous to Yemen which was a very poor country in need of financial assistance. Unemployment soared. This situation was what I found when I went to Yemen in the fall of 1991 as one of sixteen new volunteers. Three of the evacuated volunteers also returned. When war between the North and the South erupted in the spring of 1994, Peace Corps pulled its volunteers out of Yemen and has not returned. However, all the political and economic problems Yemen faced during my two-year stay in the country did not dampen my appreciation for the many wonderful experiences I had and the Yemeni friends that I made.

November 10, 1991

Hi Everyone,

I write you all as I am perched on my thin but comfortable mattress on the floor in my tiny room (about 9x7). I have a plastic wardrobe for my clothes, a small table and folding chair. Hooks on the walls and built in shelves give me places to hang and store things. Best of all is the floor to ceiling window, the top of which is made of a fan shaped stained glass. I look down onto a noisy, unpaved street busy with donkeys, children playing and throwing rocks, motorcycles, chattering men, veiled women and at night howling dogs. It is an exciting view from my window.

 I'm on the fourth floor of this 400 year old mud brick and stone hotel, known as a funduq that was originally a tower house in the Old City of Sana'a before it was converted. The panorama is amazing. I can see a mosque to my left in the distance. Beyond everything is a mountain that juts straight up several thousand feet above the city which is 7300 feet above sea level. The landscape is brown, the buildings are brown. Dust is everywhere.

The Western style bathroom, complete with toilet paper, is next door to my room. So the hotel has been modernized somewhat. The stairs are located in the center of the building, like a castle with uneven steps. There is no lighting in the stairwell. It's a hike down to the "cave" where we eat. In the cave there are two low tables surrounded by cushions on which we sit. Food is mostly vegetables, fruit and fish. We had fish in a tomato base for lunch and peppers stuffed with rice for supper. The big meal of the day is lunch, eaten around 2pm. For breakfast we're served yogurt, eggs, jams, and peanut butter!! There is always pita bread.

Because the air is so dry it is necessary to drink a lot of bottled water and tea to stay hydrated. You enter the hotel through a courtyard and low doors that require bending over so you won't hit your head.

We arrived at 2am this morning. It was a long trip, taking us three days to travel from Atlanta to Sana'a because air traffic controllers were on strike in Paris. We went to bed around 4am listening to the muezzin call for morning prayers reverberating throughout the city, hauntingly beautiful.

I feel as if I am on a movie set, part of the movie. I've never been in such a setting. A Peace Corps staffer said we're lucky to see one of the world's last frontiers before it is spoiled. Our funduq is next to a famous market known as Suq al-Milh (salt market) that has been in operation since the time the frankincense and myrrh caravans stopped here on the way to Egypt, Jerusalem, and countries bordering the Mediterranean centuries ago. Everything is sold in the suq: silver and gold jewelry, cloth, incense, jambiyas, cooking utensils, carpets, qat, and products one might find in the USA. Men wear a futa (skirt) and a belt that holds a large jambiya (curved knife). The women are covered in black from head to foot or in a patterned red and black cloth that looks like a tablecloth. Only their eyes peak through veils. Big eyed children are clothed in bright colors.

The men, both the shop owners and the customers, chew qat causing their cheeks to bulge. Qat leaves are taken from a kind of tree found only in Yemen and other countries along the southern part of the Red Sea. Chewing qat is an almost universal habit among the men. They often go to qat chews in the afternoon, and women go to their own chews as well. The Peace Corps staff will sponsor a chew for the volunteers in a couple of weeks so we can learn how to chew and the customs that are followed at a chew.

The suq is a maze of narrow streets. We ventured out into the suq today, all sixteen of us. We were afraid we would get lost and be unable to find our way back to the funduq so we decided to take all right turns and then when we returned we took all lefts. It worked.

I'm the only trainee from New England, but the country director is from Putney, VT, the cross cultural director completed his master's degree at SIT (School of International Training) in Putney. They have both gone to the horse/dog track in Hinsdale. The TEFL (Teaching English as a Second Language) coordinator is from Lynn, MA. Tomorrow classes start. This is the beginning of a big adventure. I'm excited to get started.

Getting ready for a chew   *Bean salesman*   *Dancing*

Spices in the suq

Until Next Time,

November 17, 1991

Hi Everyone,

One of the older volunteers in our group has been sick since we arrived, and because she has other medical issues, she is being sent home tomorrow. Since she will take our mail for us and post it in the States, I'm hoping you get this letter before Thanksgiving. When people travel to the States they take volunteer mail with them. This way we can be more confident that letters will arrive.

So much has happened in our first week here. We're in classes all day from 7:30 to 5:30 with just a lunch break and two other short breaks, one in the morning and one in the afternoon. Our classes include Arabic, cultural studies, and health. Later on we will receive technical training and do some practice teaching. Arabic is very difficult for me as I expected it would be and, even though I study every night for 2-3 hours, I forget what I studied by the time class starts the next day. The younger volunteers are learning Arabic faster than I am. Fridays are free from classes and mandatory meetings, like our Sundays. Often field trips are offered to anyone who wishes to go. Last Friday we traveled to Wadi Dhahr about 10 miles outside Sana'a in three Toyota Land Cruisers that the Peace Corps owns.

Dar al-Hajar

Wadi Dhahr is a wide canyon surrounded by steep cliffs. There are villages in the valley and fields of fruit trees and qat trees. Dominating the wadi is the Dar al-Hajar, a five story rock palace, perched on a rock plateau that was built as a summer residence in the 1930's for Iman Yaha who was the king in Northern Yemen from 1925 until he was assassinated in 1948. This much photographed palace is pictured in guide books and on posters that celebrate Yemen.

Wadi Dhahr is a favorite spot for Yemenis to go to celebrate special occasions. A groom was celebrating his wedding with the male members of his family and his male friends. They were dancing with jambiyas and shooting their guns into the air. A wedding celebration lasts seven days. The bride also celebrates in her home with the female members of her family and her friends.

The women volunteers went to a bride's house near the hotel to observe the celebration in her house. We went onto the roof with many of the fully veiled women to watch the groom and his party dance in the street below and listen to the unique calls of approval the women made. The bride was having henna put on her hands, arms, and the bottoms of her feet in preparation for meeting her groom for the first time near the end of the seven day celebration.

Jambiya dance

Sunday evening Muhammad, one of the Peace Corps drivers, drove the TELF coordinator, the nurse and me to the Catholic church which is a large recreational room above a grocery store located on a compound where expats in the diplomatic corps, foreign service, and employees of Hunt Oil have apartments. The Yemeni government allows a mass to be said by a priest on Sundays and special religious holidays like Christmas. Mother Theresa went to Yemen a few years ago with some of her Sisters of Charity to establish a home for orphans. Since the Sisters of Charity were doing good work for the Yemeni people, Mother Theresa said they had to have a priest to say mass. The government acquiesced to her demand even though it is illegal to practice any religion other than Islam in Yemen. The congregation is a microcosm of the foreigners living in Yemen: Europeans, Indians, Filipinos, and Americans. Going to mass makes for a very colorful event, especially on religious holidays when people wear clothes typical for going to church in their native countries. The mass is said in English by an Indian priest who came with the Sisters of Charity.

Many of the volunteers have gotten sick, mostly diarrhea, since our arrival. I've been lucky – just a mild cold. However, I'm being very careful about what I eat and drink. I even use bottled water to brush my teeth and make sure to keep my mouth closed during showers. The Yemeni staff members are very nice to us; they work us hard, but we understand why. The friendliness of the Yemeni people is wonderful. They want so much to please and show us their customs.

The other night one of our drivers took us to visit the home of two volunteers who had returned after the Gulf War. We were the first new volunteers to come to Yemen since the war ended. When the war started all the volunteers were evacuated to the States because Yemen sided with Saddam Hussein. Only three volunteers returned, the two women we visited and a male volunteer, Yaya, who converted to Islam. The women's house is in the old Jewish quarter. The Star of David was embedded in the wall over the door by law to indicate a Jewish person lived in the house. Most of the Jews left Yemen in the 1950's after the creation of Israel.

The volunteers have been invited to go to the Peace Corps Director's house to celebrate Thanksgiving. We're hoping for some turkey and beer or wine. People who have diplomatic status are allowed to ship alcohol to Yemen in the diplomatic pouch, but we don't have such a privilege and must rely on the kindness of embassy personnel to have a drink.

Happy Thanksgiving!

Celebration of a wedding continues

December 1, 1991

Dear Friends & Family,

I missed spending time with you and talking to you all at Thanksgiving. I felt so far away from everybody. I'm sure all the volunteers were feeling the same thing. We'll spend three Thanksgivings and Christmases in Yemen. Right now that seems like a long, long time to go before we return to the States. All fifteen of us went to the Peace Corps Director's house, a really nice villa, for dinner. Joe Moyer is a very nice man, and I'm sure he missed his family who are back in Vermont as his children are in school there. We all helped cook, serve and clean up. We even had a real turkey and an open bar. After dinner we went into his mafraj (living room) and sat on the floor on cushions, Yemeni style, and sang folk and Christmas songs.

The TEFL volunteers. The nurses are missing from the picture.

Being sworn in by Joe Moyer

Today, Joleen, a nurse volunteer, and I went to the Taj Sheba Hotel, a luxury hotel owned by an Indian chain, for lunch. It is way over a volunteer's budget, but we felt we needed to escape the dust and noise for a couple of hours and not worry about getting sick from the food and water. The hotel has wonderful bathrooms, a bookstore with books in English, and a beauty salon as well as the the restaurant.
So far I haven't been sick. But almost every day a new person has diarrhea. The nights are cool, in the 50's I'm guessing, and the days are nice, in the 70's and 80's. It's very dry.

Last week there was a reception for us at Joe Moyer's house. The American Ambassador, diplomats from the British and American embassies, administrators from Sana'a University were there to welcome us to Yemen.

We went on a tour of the University of Sana'a this week where some of us will be TEFL teachers. My first impression was positive, but I found out that my classes will be huge, at least 60 students in each class. Technical training has begun. The teachers are being trained to teach English as a foreign language. The nurses are receiving training to be midwives.

An American woman from the embassy is going to mail our letters for us in the States. As this opportunity seems to happen frequently, I would appreciate receiving postage stamps. Thanks for your letters. Write about the news. I feel cut off from what is happening in New Hampshire. Once a week we are given a Newsweek; I listen to the BBC and VOA (Voice of America) on a portable radio that the Peace Corps office let me borrow. If I'm lucky I find a Paris Herald Tribune that's only a week old!

A view of Sana'a from our hotel

Until next time,

December 10, 1991

Dear Family & Friends,

At last I have my computer in operating condition. I had to purchase a transformer to protect the computer because there are so many surges and blackouts that I risked damaging it if I didn't have the transformer.

It doesn't seem possible that I have been here a month. On the other hand, I feel as if I have been here for years. Every day is so long. There is so much to learn in these three months of training. Arabic has dominated most of my days and nights. As I have written before, it isn't easy for me. We are learning to write and read Arabic as well as speak it. I pretty much know the letters of the alphabet. You can imagine that my penmanship is not the greatest. Muhammad, my teacher, is very patient, but he does not like my printing! I am beginning to acquire some vocabulary, but I am by no means ready to apply for a job as a translator.

We also have a course in cross-culture. Today I had to do a report for the group on child rearing in Yemen. It went quite well, mainly because I had a lot of good discussion questions that I directed toward our Yemeni teachers. So the discussion was lively, and all I had to do was present the questions. Something that teaching taught me!!

Some of our Yemeni teachers. I couldn't take pictures of the women teachers.

Our health class is so graphic about all of the exotic diseases we might get if we are not careful that I have become quite anal about what I eat. I think I've lost a little weight, but it's hard to tell because I have to wrap myself in mounds of clothes daily in order to be culturally sensitive. When Jolene and I went to the Taj Sheba hotel for lunch recently we were both shocked to see men and women in bathing suits sitting around the pool. You don't see skin here!! But then we got over our shock when it dawned on us that the hotel is frequented by Westerners. Yemenis rarely go into the hotel. I decided not to wear a scarf when I am walking in the street. We were told that was our choice but that we had to be consistent. I will wear skirts to my ankles and mid-thigh tops with long sleeves. But always wearing a scarf is too much.

There are thirteen women in our group and two young men. Nine of the women are under thirty. Two of us are fifty. Two other women are in their early thirties. Most of the volunteers come from the West; California is the most represented. Artis, one of the young men, is from Buffalo, NY. No one else likes the Red Sox, and as might be expected, Artis is a Yankee fan.

Most of us are going to be TEFL teachers in Sana'a at the University or in an English language school. Those of us with master's degrees will be at the University. Although my classes will be huge, the good thing is that I will have no other duties: no study halls to monitor, no lunch duty, no extra-curricular activities to sponsor. Best of all, teachers are respected here. What a welcome change! The classes are very crowded as there is a big push to educate all the Yemeni children, and there are not enough teachers. Needless to say, I have a challenge ahead of me.

The old city where our hotel is located is an incredible place. The four to six story tower houses are just beautiful. They all have stained glass windows, usually in a fan shape on the top. The windows are outlined in gypsum. The top floor, the mafraj, is the best room in the house. The mafraj is where male members of the family and their guests gather to talk, chew qat, and smoke the mada'a (water pipe). Qat is a mild stimulant chewed weekly on Thursday or Friday afternoon. Those who can afford it chew daily. Chewing qat is a social thing like a cocktail party.

We had a qat chew in our mafraj two weeks ago. Our trainers taught us how to choose the best leaves, put the leaves in our mouths and chew for a while until the leaves are soft, then move them to a cheek and select new leaves to chew. By the end of the chew you have a bulging cheek. They also taught us how to smoke the mada'a that circulated around the room so that everyone could have a turn to smoke it. Personally, I found qat bitter and felt no effect. After I chewed a few times I did feel the effect and enjoyed it.

Men at a chew listening to a man playing an oud (like a lute) which is very popular in Yemen.

Typical mafraj

I'm smoking the mada'a at the Peace Corps chew.

We were told that Sana'a is one of the oldest cities in the World and that the tower houses are the World's original sky scrapers. According to folklore Sana'a was founded by Noah's son Shem. Sana'a natives often refer to the city by the nickname "Sam City" after Shem. It appears that the Western tourists are just becoming aware of the beauty of the place. Probably the neglect of this remote country by tourists is because no European nation ever colonized North Yemen. Britain occupied South Yemen. Turkey controlled parts of North Yemen but left after the fall of the Ottoman Empire. Imam Yaya, who ruled from 1925 to 1948, purposely kept Yemen isolated and backward so that he could better control the country. His son, Imam Ahmad, established Yemen's first diplomatic relations with Britain, the USA and Egypt in 1951.

I'm glad I can experience Yemen before it is spoiled by a Western invasion. Don't get me wrong. It's not easy for anyone used to American gadgets to live here. Many of the streets are unpaved in the Old City, causing a lot of dust and dirt to blow around and settle everywhere. The smells are often unpleasant. People push and shove to get where they want to go in the suq. Yep, even I was goosed the other day! The air is thin because of the altitude, and I get out of breath easily, especially when I climb the stairs in our hotel. I'm told that I will get acclimated in six weeks. Our hotel is far from plush. The electricity is off at least three times a week. We use candles at night when that happens. We have to boil our drinking water, and there always seems to be a shortage of toilet paper.

I find the Yemeni people to be friendly and fond of Americans. There has been only one anti-American demonstration since we've been here. The people seem to know the difference between the American government and the American people. President Bush is not popular because of his role in the Gulf War. Sometimes Yemeni men will say, "Bush mush taman," which means Bush is no good or Bush is bad. Over a million Yemeni workers lost their jobs in Saudi Arabia and had to leave the country because of Yemen's support of Iraq during the Gulf War. As a result of Yemen's stand, Saudi Arabia, Kuwait, and the USA have drastically cut back aid. The result of all this is that Yemen has a huge unemployment problem.

We were supposed to go on a field trip to the Ma'rib Dam that was built in the 8ᵗʰ Century BC and collapsed in 570 AD, the year Muhammad was born. The Queen of Sheba ruled in this area and traveled to meet King Solomon in Jerusalem to sign a treaty involving the caravan shipping rights with him. Peace Corps decided against our field trip because of recent hijackings of cars at gun point. When you travel outside Sana'a west toward Ma'rib, tribes rule the area. The central government has to negotiate with them when a Westerner is kidnapped. So instead of Ma'rib we went to Kawkaban and Shibam north of Sana'a. Shibam is located at the foot of Jabal (Mount) Kawkaban. When there was danger of invasion by especially the Turks, the people would climb the mountain where there is another town, Kawkaban, (now just ruins) built as a fortification for the people of Shibam. Kawkaban is very inaccessible. In the past you had to climb a steep grueling trail to reach the city on top of the mountain. Now there is a road. Thus defending themselves from an invading army was not difficult. Kawkaban is known as the city in the sky. There is a spectacular view of the area from the top. It was a rough climb, but I wasn't the last one to make it.

Shibam with Jabal Kawkaban in the background

On a recent Thursday afternoon our medical officer, a 29 year old Canadian named Marguerite, invited the women to come to her house where she had three Yemeni women ready to apply henna to our hands and feet and draw designs on our arms and paint our fingernails and toenails with a black ink. The woman who painted me I had met before. She is the mother of Ali, one of our Arabic teachers. I was invited to go to their house for lunch one day. I guess she liked me because she wants me to become her husband's second wife. What a proposal! She painted my hands and feet up just fine. It will take six months for the henna to disappear.

Henna being applied by wife # 1   *The result*

In spite of my long eventful days here, I get a little homesick at times, but I know that's natural given the situation. It would be great if I could take a long weekend break to visit you. When you are so far from home, family and friends take on a new meaning. I can get along without my gadgets, but I miss everyone very much.

So from the land of the Three Wise Men I wish you a Merry Christmas. We are going to go to the Red Sea city of Al-Hudayda for three days at Christmas, but I'll be with you in spirit.

Until Next Time,

January 11, 1992

Happy New Year Everyone,

I'm thinking of you all in the midst of winter storms and very cold weather. When I called my parents on New Year's Day it was 6 below zero at their house. I'll take the mild winter of Sana'a thank you very much. I've only seen two short rain showers since I've been here. I hope the summers won't be beastly, but I'm told that although the summers are hot, the heat won't be too bad. The dry air and altitude help with that. My skin is drying out like mad and my hair has no body. Speaking of hair, for those of you who are curious, it's coming in white. In a couple of months my real color will be all that you will see in pictures.

Al-Hudayda

We spent Christmas in Al-Hudayda. It is a nice resort city on the Red Sea. Now don't think it is the Ritz. Remember where I am. But it is a beautiful setting with a nice green central park, stunning harbor, wonderful fresh fish and some pleasant hotels to hang out in where you can actually get a beer! I spent a lovely afternoon on the covered roof top of our hotel with a beautiful view of the sea while the other volunteers went swimming. It was a smart choice because many of my friends came back with bad sun burns and were in agony the next day. I wrote lesson plans and enjoyed the salt air while I ate a nice lunch. In the middle of the afternoon a waiter brought me some qat to chew. I enjoyed it and the spectacular sun setting over the Red Sea.

Fishing boat on the Red Sea

The bus trip to Al-Hudayda was incredible. We drove down a narrow twisting road through the mountains, past terraced fields, flocks of sheep, shepherds, and heavily burdened donkeys. We passed villages perched on mountain slopes. When we reached the Tihama (desert) we saw camels and circular houses made out of reeds. The African influence was very obvious. As the people dress like Biblical characters, it was quite a moving Christmas pageant. I've learned to accept the wild Yemeni drivers who don't slow down for curves, just pull into the on-coming lane and say, "in shaa'al-laah" (if Allah wills it). I let the bus driver drive and I admired the view.

The Road to Al-Hudayda

January 12, 1992

Hi Again Everyone,

We're right in the middle of practice teaching now. Our students are also volunteers from a school in Sana'a. Their ages range from about 16 to mid-20's. The competition to be selected into the program was stiff. 120 were accepted to make up three classes of 40 each. 150 were turned away. The students get no credit for taking the six week course. They have to come to class for three hours daily from 3 to 6. Three of us are assigned to a class, and we teach for an hour each. Can you imagine American students sitting for three hours with only one ten minute break? But they are enthusiastic, eager to learn English. They are amazing rote learners. If you teach them a dialogue or read them a story they quickly put it to memory. But on the flip side, these students don't know what to do with a thought question, an opinion question or an inference question. The other day I was trying to get them to vote on the best title for a story I read to them. They wouldn't vote! It's foreign to them. Last names are not used. My teacher name is Miss Mary. They just won't add the "Lou".

Yesterday one of the teachers was playing a guessing game with the students about famous people. One student chose Saddam Hussein as his famous person to describe. He referred to him as the hero of Arab people because he stood up to the Western World. We're told to stay out of politics, but it's everywhere just below the surface.

By the way NEVER COMPLAIN ABOUT THE CLEANLINESS OF PUBLIC BATHROOMS AGAIN! You ain't seen nothin'. We could only find one bathroom in the school. As you approach the hallway where it is, the smell is overpowering. I stuck my head in the other day just to see what it was like. I gaged. We all hope we'll never have to use it. Most toilets here are Turkish. My thigh muscles are getting stronger every day, especially after my recent bout of diarrhea.

At the end of the month we will be sworn in as Peace Corps Volunteers, and I'll begin my job at Sana'a University. It is not known when the semester will begin because it hasn't been decided yet. Nor is it known when the semester will end.

Ramadan begins sometime the end of February. Nothing much gets done in schools or at work during that month we are told. After the swearing in we'll be moving into our own places in Sana'a or to a village somewhere. The nurses will become midwives in clinics in remote areas of Yemen.

I've had a shot for about everything imaginable: typhoid, hepatitis B, rabies, tetanus, polio, yellow fever, meningitis, measles, and diphtheria. We have to take malaria pills for a month because Al-Hudayda is in a malaria zone. We spend a lot of time talking about our digestive systems. We have to be very careful of the water because all fresh water here is contaminated with either the snail that causes schistosomiasis which is endemic in Yemen or is contaminated with "poop" as we affectionately call it. Human feces are used as fertilizer so washing vegetables and fruits is very important. Don't eat it if you don't cook it or peel it is the saying. Sometimes these are difficult rules to follow. When you are a guest in a Yemeni home you have to be polite. I've been very careful about what I eat, but I still connected with some kind of bacteria and had diarrhea for a week. Experienced staff members just laugh at us rookies because this kind of problem is part of the Peace Corps experience. At the moment I'm enjoying constipation.

We were invited to a couple of parties at Christmas. Our medical officer had a Christmas Eve party for us, a sit-on-the floor dinner. You always sit on the floor to eat. The American Ambassador had an open house at the embassy for the American community. We sang carols and ate. Peace Corps volunteers are always noticeable because they hang out at the food table and open bar. We are the poor relations of the ex-pat community with no diplomatic pouch privileges. There are many American business people in Yemen. Many of them work for the Texas Hunt Oil Company. But I feel proud that we're not in Yemen to make money or spy for the CIA. I know I wouldn't want to live this way indefinitely. I do remember my microwave with affection. But it's good for the soul to live without the "things" for the time being.

We are all looking for houses and apartments. Three of us got a nice downstairs unfurnished duplex yesterday. There is nothing in the house except a bathroom and sink fixtures. We'll have to get a stove, refrigerator, dishes, beds, everything! It has a walled in yard with flowers and a Western bathroom. We each have our own bedroom and share a kitchen and mafraj. We will swear in January 30th and move on the 31st. My address will be the same at the Peace Corps office, and I will have a telephone, so you can call. I won't be able to make long distant calls. I'll let you all know what my number is.

My best to you all,

January 25, 1992

Hi Everyone,

Only six more days and boot camp will finally be over! I got your letter mailed January 13th today Mom and Dad. Only 12 days. Not bad. It's funny that sometimes mail arrives fairly promptly, but I'm still getting mail sent in December. The good news is that it does seem to arrive eventually.

We're getting ready to move into the house I mentioned in my last letter. My housemates will be Beth, a 22 year old recent University of Michigan graduate from Michigan, and Fran, a 60 plus retired teacher from Ohio. Peace Corps makes for strange bedfellows. The landlords live upstairs, and we have the ground floor. The husband works in a bank and has traveled to the States. Our rent is 5000 riyals a month. On the black market a dollar is worth 29 riyals, today, so that is somewhere around $175 to $200 a month. I will have 4400 riyals to live on after I pay my share of 2000 toward the rent. The black market is the true economic measure of the riyal's worth. The government's official rate is 12 riyals to the dollar.

The house is surrounded by a 10 to 12 foot wall that will give us privacy. Our private entrance opens into a small tiled courtyard with flower gardens on either side. A veranda goes the length of the house. The sun shines every day so I'll be able to enjoy sitting outside in my shorts. I want to plant an herb garden and some more flowers. The soil is mainly clay so I don't know how they will do.

A hall goes the length of the house. All the rooms open off this hall: a kitchen, bath with a Western toilet, mafraj, and three bedrooms. My room is about 18 by 12. Huge! It has three windows and a tiny closet where I can put folded things on shelves, but I don't know yet how I am going to hang things. I went to the suq the other day and bargained in ARABIC for Yemeni wool rugs. I bought a long narrow one about 14 by 4 and two 6 by 2 runners for 2000 riyals (about $70). They will be good to have in my room to protect me from the cold stone floor. They weren't expensive until you remember that I'm earning about $250.00 a month. I must learn to think in riyals, not dollars. I also bought a large brass tray and a brass perfume holder for about $22.00 and some Indian cashmere cloth for a wall hanging for about $10.00. The Yemeni cloth seems to look cheap and unattractive compared to the Indian cloth. But I'm just beginning to look. We bought our mattresses in the suq and carried them back on our heads. We bought a small refrigerator (dorm room size) because we couldn't afford a big one. The big ones we looked at seemed huge, almost obscene. I found a table and chair for my computer and a cloth (futa) to cover it to protect it from the dirt. We found a three burner gas hot plate that will serve as our stove. We will have to have mafraj cushions made.

My finished room

I love to walk through the suq as I've mentioned before. It's really one of my favorite things to do. However, it's a pain dealing with some men who grab women who are not veiled. In the last two weeks my right breast has been fondled and I've been grabbed in the crotch. So I bought a three foot long flexible stick that is used to drive donkeys. I carry it with me, and the next grabber will get to feel the sting of my stick. It's forbidden to treat women this way so I will not be in trouble using the stick for protection.

We're excited to have a phone and hope to receive calls from the States soon. We can't make calls because it doesn't have an international line. My phone number is (011-967-1-78094).
This letter is being mailed by my TEFL coordinator who is returning to the states to have her baby in Boston. As she says, the baby would be an American where ever he's born, but the only way he can be a New Englander is to be born one!

That's it for now folks.

Until next time,

February 4, 1992

Hi Everyone,

Greetings from my new house somewhere in Sana'a. I don't have a street address as the street I live on is nameless as far as we can ascertain. It's fun trying to explain where we want to go to taxi drivers, but I guess this is not an unusual thing here.

Our landlords live upstairs. The walls and floors are so thick in this house that you can't hear any noise from upstairs. The day we moved in we went upstairs to pay our 5000 riyals for a month's rent. We sat with the wife and daughters on the floor in their mafraj to sign and fill out rent receipts. They served us a punch drink that Fran and I didn't want to drink as we suspected that it wasn't made with boiled water, but ceremony demanded that we be polite and drink it, so we did. No ill effects.

We are still waiting for our butagas (gas tank like one used with a grill) so that we can cook. There is a waiting list for butagas tanks in Sana'a that sell for 1500 riyals on the black market. Peace Corps will be able to get them for us for 500 riyals. But, as with all bureaucracies, it takes time. Why they didn't order the butagas for us earlier we can't understand. The good news is that we have one of the best bakeries in Sana'a in our neighborhood. We love their kudam, a wheat round bread, very hearty and delicious, known here as soldiers' bread. We live five minutes from the Peace Corps Office, making it convenient to get our mail and find out the news.

As I think I wrote before, my salary is 6400 riyals a month. The official government rate of exchange is 12 riyals to the dollar. This is the rate our government recognizes when they give Yemen dollars for our salaries. That would mean that my salary is about $533 a month. The back market rate of exchange is around 29 riyals to the dollar. In Yemen the real economy is based on the black market rate. So in reality I only earn $220 per month give or take. Still, I can pay my share of the rent and live quite well. We joke that the Yemen Government probably takes the US dollars and exchanges them on the black market!

We were sworn in as official volunteers on January 29th at the Peace Corps Director's house. Our trainers, American and British embassy officials, and Yemeni officials were there to witness the swearing in. I gather that swearing-in ceremonies used to be more elaborate, but the Peace Corps budget for Yemen has been cut back. The budget was so tight at the end of training that they had to cut down on food for us. We especially resented the lack of oranges in our diets. Yemen isn't on good terms with the US government because of the Gulf War. Whether or not that translates into a cut back on oranges for us is impossible to tell, but we laughingly say so anyway. At one time, there were well over 50 volunteers here. Now there are 18, 15 new ones and 3 who returned after the Gulf War.

The Peace Corps push appears to be to send volunteers to Eastern Europe. Funny, that's where I wanted to go when I signed up, but now I feel so lucky to be in Yemen. I am living in a medieval culture with token rays of modern conveniences. I still think I'll wake up to find it's all a dream. Veiled women and men in futas with big jambiyas around their waists are all looking very normal to me as is the sound of the five calls to prayer every day. We're even thinking of hosting our own qat chew soon.

My teaching job at the University will begin in about a week. Classes won't start, but we are going to do a lot of curriculum planning during February at the Peace Corps office. Classes begin March 7th, I guess. March is Ramadan, and Islamic countries come to a standstill. From morning call to prayer to evening call to prayer no one can eat, drink, smoke, have sex or swallow saliva. People are up all night indulging in all that is forbidden during the day. It's a festive time with qat chews and friends and families visiting one another. Stores are open all night and people are out and about. I'm looking forward to observing what goes on during Ramadan. We're told that students don't faithfully attend classes during this time so it will be a strange way to begin the semester. I'll write you about all this when I observe it firsthand. The Old University, where I'll be teaching, is about a 20 minute walk from our house so I'll continue to get exercise.

We walked to the center of town today, only a ten minute walk. We really do have an excellent location. About everywhere we want to go is 10 to 15 minutes from our house. Taxis are not expensive – about 25 riyals for the average ride in Sana'a, less than a dollar by black market prices. But now I'm earning riyals and so must think in riyals. 30 riyals is beginning to seem like a lot of money. We went to the British Council which has an excellent library. We joined for 150 riyals for the year in order to be able to borrow books. The setting is lovely, nice reading rooms and a quiet courtyard. We are all delighted to have access to this library. The Peace Corps office has a library, too, but it is not as extensive as the one at the British Council.

Until next time,

(picture is of me at swearing-in)

February 15, 1992

Greetings to One and All,

Old City of Sana'a

Today had an exciting beginning as my brother Jim, Cyndy and Lindsay called me at 7am (11pm in New Hampshire). It was so wonderful to hear their voices which were very clear as if they were just a couple of miles away. My niece Meagan is on a school trip in France. I'm so excited for her because France is an exciting place to be.

Our curriculum work has been very laid back. We work at the Peace Corps office for three hours every morning. We're going through text books and workbooks trying to find exercises, drills, explanations and simple reading passages to photocopy and make into a text book for us to use at the University to teach English as a foreign language. The English Department at the University will make copies and sell them to our students. As Yemen hasn't signed the international copyright agreement, it isn't illegal to do this, but it does seem strange as if we are doing something very wrong. There are two problems with the English textbooks here: the University can't or won't buy published textbooks and, secondly, most of the TEFL material that is available is written by the British. A lot of the material is a hard core sell of British culture and history. Some of the material is also not culturally sensitive for use in Yemen. For example, many textbooks have reading passages about drinking whisky in bars or male/female relationships that are forbidden here. We have to be very careful about what teaching materials we use as the University is very conservative. The Muslim Brotherhood is growing stronger, and there have been problems with teaching materials in the past. It would be great if an American company would write TEFL/ESL materials for use in the Middle East that are culturally sensitive and not written mainly to promote American culture. Our classes are going to be very basic: vocabulary, simple grammar and writing. I will even have to teach the alphabet and how to write the letters.

I am healthier than I've been in a long time. I walk everywhere now so a one or two mile walk is nothing. My diet is simple and healthy. I have lost 20 pounds and my cholesterol level has dropped. My back isn't bothering me either. I think the hysterectomy I had before leaving for Yemen took care of that problem.

This morning I washed my sheets in the bathtub, and they are now drying on the line we strung on the veranda. It's a pain to wash this way. There is a convenient laundry right around the corner. They wash clothes by hand and iron them. Shirts cost 7 riyals, pants and skirts 10 riyals. So it's real cheap and they do a nice job. However, you can walk by the place and see your laundry hanging over the street to dry. For that reason I do my underwear by hand. I can't be without the sheets for the two days it takes them to do my laundry because I only have one pair of unfitted sheets; I have yet to find fitted sheets here.

The other day we found a coffee filter so, finally, we can have decent coffee. I wish I had my coffee grinder and coffee maker here. What I wouldn't give for a trip to Sam's/BJ's right now. We all wish we could pack one suitcase with things from home that we wish we had. One thing I'm very glad I have, however, is this computer. It makes writing these letters so much easier.

I went to a Hunt Oil Company party the other night. The person hosting it has a lovely apartment in the "compound" where the diplomats and oil people live. There was great food and an open bar. It was like being home for a while. Most of the people there were either British or American. I particularly enjoyed talking baseball with a man from Maine who was a pitcher for the University of Maine. Of course he is a Red Sox fan. We compared thoughts on the up-coming season and shared Red Sox agonies from the past. People come here to work in the oil fields for a year or two to make some good money, save it, and then return home with their nest eggs. The life of a Peace Corps Volunteer is so different.

Tomorrow I might go to Aden and Ta'izz with a couple of other volunteers and Barbara Ferris, the Peace Corps director for women in the developing countries. I spent the day yesterday showing her around Sana'a and the suq. She will be speaking soon at the UN about women's issues in the Developing World. We won't find out until tomorrow if we will be allowed to go.

That's it for now,

Qat sellers in the suq

Bab al-Yemen (the gateway or door to the Suq in the Old City of Sana'a)

February 21, 1992

Greetings former Hinsdale colleagues,

Sorry about the group letter. I try to keep up with my correspondence, but the cost of mailing a letter is becoming a factor as I don't have the number of opportunities to send letters back to the states with Americans anymore. I figure you can run off a copy or two as needed. Also, I find that I am saying the same thing in every letter. I will try to answer the questions some of you have raised.

At the moment I am on semi-vacation. Training ended the end of January, and we moved into our own houses/apartments right after the swearing in. It has become my job to water the plants (mostly cacti and rubber plants). I want to get some roses to plant, but they are expensive, and I need to get used to working with this clay-like soil first. I planted some zinnias and morning glories which couldn't poke their heads through the hard soil! My brother is mailing a package to me with herbs and tomato seeds. I'm going to buy potting soil, clay pots and try to get the plants started before subjecting them to Yemeni soil. I think one of the problems is that there has been a drought here since 1987 and people don't put anything back into the soil. I refuse to gather human fertilizer to mix with the soil. That is a major source of fertilizer here.

By the way, dogs are not pets here. Muhammad considered them unclean animals so Islam has a negative attitude toward them. Yemenis would never have them as pets, allow them in their houses and cannot understand why Americans keep them as pets. There are dogs here. They roam in packs at night throughout the city. You can hear them howling. Cats are pets sometimes, but many of them in Sana'a are rabid. That's why we have had to have three rabies shots. Anyway, as our house is walled in, I don't have anything to worry about.

I just came back from a two hour walk by myself around Sana'a. I went to the Suq to buy another brass candle stick holder at my favorite brass spot. On the way, I passed through the vegetable suq. I noticed that there were many herbs for sale. I have been looking for fresh basil for a long time. I wasn't sure if the plant I looked at was basil, didn't know the name for basil in Arabic, so I decided to give it the old sniff test. Well. The vender threw the leaf away after I sniffed it! Gasp! I guess I sucked the essence out of it. It is funny about what is not acceptable in other cultures. You are not supposed to blow your nose in public or eat with your left hand here. But you can pick your nose and make a lot of noise while you are eating.

Yemeni woman carrying goods

Let me answer your questions about Turkish toilets. They are made out of porcelain with a hole about 4 to 6 inches in diameter and are flat on the floor. The object is to aim everything into the hole, which takes practice. Toilet paper is not used by the Yemenis. Usually a little rubber hose attached to a cold water faucet is next to the toilet, sort of a crude bidet. Anyway that's why it's impolite to eat with your left hand. Actually, they are often cleaner than public western toilets and aren't hard to use once you get used to them.

However, I'm happy to report that our house has a Western toilet. We cannot flush paper down the toilet, however, as the ancient, questionable sewage system can't handle paper; we empty the pail containing the toilet paper into the local dumpster every day. In past times (I don't know if it still goes on) the five story tower houses were equipped with a bathroom on each floor. The waste would be sent to the basement of the house. There it would dry out and, periodically, someone would gather it and sell it to farmers who would fertilize their crops with it. Because it is so dry here, the urine would run down the wall only part way before it evaporated. Human waste is still used as fertilizer, and that is the reason why we have to be so careful about cleaning fruits and vegetables. We have to soak anything that is not peeled or cooked in boiled water and bleach for 20 minutes.

Many of you asked about shopping. Well, let me tell you it is an experience. Everywhere there are little stores called dukans. You know it is a store because it has a blue door. The shops are very small and carry only a few things. In the suq you can buy fruits, vegetables, meat, fish, and poultry. People buy live chickens, carry them home and cook them for dinner. I never expect to do that! There is a lot of lamb and goat here. In the meat market they put the head of the animal for sale with the blood and guts on the counter so you'll know what you are buying. There is, of course, an abundance of flies. I think I'll become a vegetarian!

The suq in the Old City

The bread here is wonderful. We have a little bakery just across the street. They sell fresh pita bread and a bread called kudam. The bread is made in brick ovens. I realize that I had never eaten good pita before coming to Yemen. It costs one riyal for each piece. You go into the bakery, pick up your warn loaves, wrap them in day-old newspapers and take them home. The bread is great for sandwiches or just plain. You buy fresh bread for every meal. I eat a lot of tuna fish and peanut butter. There are some supermarkets here, but they are very small like a 7-eleven. You can sometimes find American products, but they are expensive and the date for selling has long since expired. I eat out a lot.

For lunch we often eat the national dish, salta. The main ingredient is hulba (fenugreek), chopped meat and spices, eaten with pita bread that you use to dip into the boiling hot mixture. Forks and spoons are not used. Everything is eaten with hands and bread. I also eat decka which is chopped meat and spices eaten with bread. Two other favorites are bean dishes, ful and fasula, also made with spices. They are quite good actually. There are little hole-in-the-wall restaurants everywhere. You can get one of the above mentioned dishes for between 20 to 30 riyals with bread and tea or soda. You don't tip here except in exclusive restaurants. Before you eat and after you eat it is polite to wash your hands in the little sink because people dip into the same dish. I always think I'm pouring more germs onto my hands as the water is so contaminated. Some of these restaurants are on the other side of clean. A couple of weeks ago I was eating my ful when a cockroach walked across the table beside my dish. I told him to get lost, but he didn't understand English. We often eat gyros here, called swammers, that are sold on the street for five riyals apiece. Perhaps you understand now why I've lost weight.

Eating salta with friends

There are so many images I wish I could adequately share with you; men in long zennas and jambiyas, often carrying machine guns, holding hands with other men (women and men don't hold hand in public), fully veiled women with only their shoes and sometimes their eyes showing. Teachers recognize their female students by their shoes! In the afternoons men look as if they have golf balls in their cheeks as they are chewing qat. In the streets I see donkeys and sheep as well as cars and trucks. In all directions around Sana'a there are spectacular mountains.

We are on alert at the moment because of the Lebanon situation. There are banners and demonstrations. We're just supposed to stay out of crowds. I mainly go out when they are chewing qat in the afternoon. They are pretty mellow then. The scenes bear no resemblance to any other scenes I've witnessed in the Middle East. We're told that Yemen is more conservative, more traditional than many other Arab countries. During Ramadan, which begins the first of March, we won't be able to eat or drink in public because it wouldn't be polite. Anyway, all the restaurants and stores will be closed during the day until evening call to prayer.

The first of March I will begin working at the University full time. We have to buy all our classroom materials including chalk and erasers. Thanks so much for your letters. I enjoy hearing what is happening in New Hampshire. I keep up on the World news through my weekly copy of Newsweek that Peace Corps gives us.

Keep the letters coming,

March 3, 1992

Hi Everyone,

I have become particularly interested in the bakery near us where we buy wonderful kudam and pita bread. Recently, when I have gone in, I have looked around and tried to talk to the two workers who are always there, an old man with a white beard who appears to be the chief baker as he is the one who puts the bread in the oven and determines when it should come out, and a younger man who works with the dough, forming it into kudam size pieces. When it is cooked, it is about six inches in diameter and a little thicker than pita bread, like an oversized hamburger roll.

Yesterday I watched the old man put the bread in the oven using very long paddles. The brick and stone oven is probably fueled by gas as wood is scarce. I had to bend over to look through the small semi-circular opening. The flat surface inside was made of stone, and the heat was very intense. The young man told me that the dough is made early in the morning, obviously giving it time to rise. The dough was in a rectangular wooden frame (5' x 3'). I looked at the large bags of wheat flour at the side of the room. Guess where they came from? The USA! It struck me as ironic that our farmers produce good wheat flour that is shipped to the developing world where it's made into delicious bread, the like of which is hard to find in the USA.

I have come to the conclusion that the more technologically advanced a country is the worse its bread is (the exception of course is France). Our super markets are loaded with dozens of bread choices, but not one loaf competes with this magnificent kudam that the poorest of Yemenis eat daily. At home we are so pleased if we find a bakery that makes decent bread, and will travel out of our way especially to buy good bread. Here excellent bread is everywhere, even in the simplest hole-in-the-wall restaurants. I hope if I'm patient and they become comfortable with me that I can go some morning when they make the dough.

Last weekend we found good coffee beans on Hadda Street. The dark beans are like espresso beans and too strong for everyday coffee. The light beans are too mild. So we mixed them, half a kilo of each, and had the man grind them coarser than they usually do. Usually their coffee is like dust and will go through the finest filter. So now every morning I'm finally enjoying a real cup of coffee. It's ironic that the good mocha coffee originally came from Yemen before some coffee plants were pirated away to Java where the same coffee is now produced in abundance. The Yemenis drink a lot of tea with an unbelievable amount of sugar in each cup. The lush coffee fields have been slowly disappearing, giving way to the more lucrative qat crop. Unfortunately for the economy, qat is not exported for two reasons. First of all it is very perishable. It has to be chewed soon after picking. Secondly, some countries outlaw it; the USA, for one, prohibits the import of qat. The rumor is that it is smuggled across the border into Saudi Arabia for illegal consumption there, including the king who chews it as a way of controlling his weight. Qat retards the appetite. Most of the qat produced is consumed in Yemen. The country would be much better off economically if it were exporting coffee as it would bring foreign revenue into Yemen. The health issue is also a factor. Although the Yemenis maintain that it is only a mild stimulant similar to coffee, some people feel that it is still unknown what the health effects really are. One thing known for certain is that chewing qat has a negative effect on pregnant women because they fail to eat properly and infants are born tiny and often remain malnourished if the nursing mother chews instead of eating. Some enlightened Yemenis are aware of these negative effects, but chewing qat is such a part of daily life it would be extremely difficult to outlaw it.

My personal news is good, but I've been worried for a few weeks that I would be medevac'd to Washington. Blood was found in my stool and the medical officer panicked and contacted Washington. The blood was first noticed during training when I had that week long session with diarrhea. Marguerite, the medical officer, had me submit other samples after I moved into the house. They were all positive. Washington ordered a barium enema which I had the joy of experiencing a few days ago. I will ask you to use your imaginations concerning this chapter of my adventure.

I sat in a waiting room, squatting on the floor part of the time with a large group of Yemenis, the men chewing qat, drinking water and smoking, the women fully veiled, waiting for the Indian technician. When it was finally my turn I was asked to climb onto the normal looking table you would find in an x-ray room. BUT THERE WAS NO SHEET ON THE WOODEN TABLE. I thought it was strange that she didn't want me to undress and put on a jonnie. But she motioned for me to remove my shoes. Her English was even more limited than my Arabic. So as I had no previous knowledge of this exam to fall back on, I did as she wished. She pulled up my shirt and yanked up my bra to the middle of my breasts. OUCH! As I was lying on my back I couldn't unhook my bra. It wasn't a pretty picture. The tube kept slipping out and the liquid sprayed all over everything. My clothes were soaked. Marguerite yelled, "Squeeze your buttocks, Mary Lou,"

When she was finished then she gave me a jonnie. I undressed and had to scurry across a public hallway, after she chased the men away, to the bathroom. Guess what, no toilet paper. I opened the door and called to Marguerite who brought me some tissues so I could clean up. The toilet, minus the seat, looked as if it hadn't been washed in a week or so. Again it's a good thing I've learned to squat. Naturally the toilet wouldn't flush as the water had been turned off. I had to use my plumbing knowledge to find the shut-off valve and turn on the water, which just trickled in. I went to the sink to wash my hands and found a large rock peacefully resting in it. All the time I was there I kept saying to myself, "You must be flexible, Mary Lou."

As medicine is so primitive here and the sterile conditions poor at best, Marguerite wouldn't allow me to have an upper GI series or the good old scope exploration. She originally had told me that she was sure Washington would want both done because of my age and they wouldn't want to take any chances. I was mentally preparing myself for an early exit from Yemen and was more than a little disappointed. But to come to the good news, the x-rays showed a perfectly lovely posterior, not a sign of a problem. A re-testing of my stool showed it to be perfectly normal. My blood work is great. Probably just a fluke caused by diet or the vitamin pill I was taking that can cause constipation. They are going to follow up every couple of months with additional stool sample tests just to make sure. But I know I'm healthy. I feel too good to have anything seriously wrong.

During this whole investigation I had to go to the American Embassy to see the American doctor for a checkup. Security is so tight. All kinds of identification is needed to get onto Embassy grounds. Pocketbooks are checked. You have to have a confirmed appointment. Sad. I remember the days when you could just open the door of an American Embassy and walk in.

Ramadan has begun. It started here a day later than it did in Saudi Arabia. The mornings are very quiet, like the middle of the night. People are asleep unless they have jobs they have to go to. All the stores and restaurants are closed. In the late afternoon stores begin to open so that people can buy food and prepare for the evening meal that is eaten once the call is heard announcing sunset. At around 8 pm, life begins in the streets. It's like daytime. The suq is busy, businesses open and people begin to socialize. Everyone stays up most of the night. Life is turned upside down. Everyone is supposed to be kind to beggars and their fellowmen during this holy month. It is supposed to be safe to walk by yourself at night, just like the day. I went out last night and walked for an hour from 8 to 9. It was strange to see all the life going on in darkness. I felt safer than I usually would walking at night. I was surprised about the comments I got. I don't know what most of them were, but I know I received a lot of anti-American comments. Everyone was walking around in groups and intoxicated with the celebration. I expect that's why people spoke harshly to me; you know the courage of a mob. Anyway, I was glad I had my stick with me. I won't go out alone at night again; it's definitely a group activity.

Today we started to register students for the second semester at the University. I waited in my assigned room for the 60 students to show up. Only twelve made it for each class. All I had to do was to check their student ID's and have them sign up for class. The ones who showed up seemed very nice, and I was excited to meet them. It has been a long time getting to this point. I have to go every day this week to meet the students who show up. Because it is Ramadan, most of them will not show up to register or attend classes until April. No one knows for sure what will happen. There are also strike rumors because the Yemeni president, Ali Abdullah Salah, visited the University and somehow insulted the professors. If they strike, we won't go either. Anyway, it is a casual way to begin my teaching career at Sana'a University.

View from my classroom

My classroom is large. It looks out onto the central courtyard with shrubs and trees in bloom in one direction and onto a parking lot in the other direction. Today was hot, but the classroom was nice and cool. The students I talked to speak English about as well as I speak Arabic (meaning hardly literate) so my teaching will be very basic.

All the Peace Corps volunteers are assigned to the College of Arts. We work for the language center teaching students from various departments. Mine come from the history, Islamic and Arabic Studies, geography, psychology and philosophy departments. They all have to take English. It is a University requirement. I'll be teaching two classes a day, three hours total. All together I have five classes, 60 students in each class. But each class only meets twice a week. We don't have classes Thursday or Friday. My earliest class twice a week is at 10. Twice a week I don't go until 12. On Tuesdays my first class is at 2PM. Classes are over at 5:30. My two daily classes are back to back except on Monday. I have to hang out a bit at the language center and get to know other staff members and to be available for students who need help. Other than that I have no responsibilities at the University. We won't be giving homework as the classes are too large. The only tests are the midterm and the final which all of us will write and administer together. Once I'm adjusted to everything I don't expect it will be too taxing. I think it will be fun. The students are so warm and friendly. Teachers are very much respected, and of course as an American I am somewhat exotic.

Once I'm settled into teaching, I'll be expected to get involved with a secondary project. I would like to get involved somehow with a women's group that is trying to advance women's education. Did you read the March 9th Newsweek? Exciting work is beginning in the developing world with women. Barbara Ferris, who visited us here, is involved with that work. She encouraged us to get involved with women's groups in Yemen.

I just returned from the bakery. During Ramadan you can't get bread until 6PM. So at 6:30 I went to get some. My young friend was there by himself. He invited, I should say, insisted, that I share some salta with him. He gave me a fresh kudam roll and I joined him eating from the same bowl. Salta is the North Yemen luncheon dish made with hulba (fenugreek). I really don't particularly like it as fenugreek is such a foreign taste for me. I can't describe it as I don't know what to compare it to. I suspect that you have to acquire a taste for it. But I was thrilled by the honor of his invitation. I thought it was a good time to ask if I could watch him make the dough. He told me that during Ramadan dough is made at 1pm and that I could watch. So I'm going to go next Thursday, my day off.

I must get these letters off to the woman who is returning to the States and has volunteered to mail our letters. As always I think of you all and thank you for your letters. I just heard yesterday that Mrs. Yawkey died. Is it true? Please give details. What's happening with the Sox?

My best to all,

Medevac'd to Washington, DC, around March 20, 1992

Peace Corps Washington did not accept the results of my barium enema in Sana'a because they thought the test was inconclusive and ordered my return to Washington for more complete testing.

Before I left Yemen, I had to make out a "will" specifying what would happen to my worldly goods in Yemen if I were not able to return. I packed lightly because I hoped to return and wanted room in my luggage to bring more stuff back with me. This time I was the one to carry everyone's mail.

On the first stage of my journey I arrived in Rome where I had to go through customs and change planes. The custom inspectors gave me a thorough search because I had come from Yemen, and I guess they feared I might be a terrorist or carrying a bomb unknowingly for a terrorist. They were particularly interested in the folder where the travel agent had placed my ticket because something was written in Arabic on it. They kept grilling me about the Arabic writing. I could tell them nothing. I didn't know what it said or who had written it there. Finally, after having me turn on my laptop and seeing that didn't blow up, they let me board the plane that was delayed because of me. They told me they were keeping my luggage in order to give it a thorough search and that they would deliver it to my hotel in Washington the next day, which they did.

The small hotel in Virginia, just outside Washington, was reserved for Peace Corps Volunteers who were medevac'd to the States. Volunteers were coming back with all kinds of illnesses not usually found in the USA. I shared a room with a legally blind volunteer from Eastern Europe. I can't remember what her health problem was.

I was assigned a nurse who was in charge of arranging for my tests and transportation to and from George Washington University Hospital where medevac'd Peace Corps Volunteers were evaluated and treated. For over a week I went daily to the hospital for tests on about every part of my body and saw all kinds of doctors including a dermatologist. On the weekend I was in Washington, I was allowed to go stay with friends in Washington since no tests were scheduled. The end result was that the only thing wrong with me that they could find were some small hemorrhoids that didn't bother me. The nurse assigned to me said it was a good thing that they found the hemorrhoids, otherwise I would not be allowed to return to Yemen.

I was given permission to fly to New Hampshire to see friends and family for a week. I stayed with my brother for a few days and went shopping at Sam's where I bought some precious fitted sheets and other items that I would find useful in Yemen. This was every volunteer's dream to be able to go shopping in the States for things you wished you had with you in Yemen. The rest of the week I spent with my parents. A friend picked me up and drove me to Boston where I caught a flight back to Washington and began my long journey back to Sana'a.

My journey took me through Frankfort, Germany, where I changed planes. I noticed that many of the women on the plane put their veils, head scarfs and abayas on once we left Frankfort and got closer to Yemen. When we left Yemen and headed for Rome on my trip to the States, they removed their abayas, head scarfs and veils once we neared Rome.

I arrived back in Sana'a very exhausted after almost 24 hours of travel. A Peace Corps driver picked me up at the airport and drove me home. My little mattress on the floor was a welcome sight!

April 17, 1992

Dear family and friends,

This Good Friday finds me back in Sana'a for a week and a half since my trip to the USA. As I write this letter, many images of home swirl in my mind. But as I predicted when I was there, it all seems surreal, almost as if I wasn't there. I saw so many people, had so many conversations in such a short space that for me it was a little overwhelming. Remember, I was trying to get used to shinny shoes and powerfully flushing toilets. However, I am glad I got to see as many of you as I did and regret not seeing many others.

School began for me on Saturday morning. I found out what I was supposed to teach five minutes before class started as no one had left me any plans or a summary of what had been covered in my absence. So I began my teaching experience in Sana'a "winging it." A couple of my classes are full – sixty students is the maximum number we will take. That doesn't mean that all of them show up, usually only half of them do. Students are still registering for my other three classes. We're going to give a mid-term the beginning of May and a final the end of May or the beginning of June. You can imagine that it must be a little chaotic. All the same, I'm enjoying my classes. The students, especially the men, are lively and curious. I wish the women would speak up more, but they are dealing with societal restraints. They always sit on house right and the men on house left. The aisle separates them. I really don't expect I'll ever learn their names as all I see are their eyes. Many of them even wear gloves during class. I am, of course, a curiosity because I am an American woman.

I was wondering what it was going to be like on the 15th when sanctions began against Libya. So far, no comments. In one class this week when I was having them write about their hometowns, a Palestinian student wrote about wishing his enemies would get out of his country and that American soldiers would go home. So far I have discovered no comment seems to work best even if I happen to agree personally with the comment expressed. Politics is potentially an explosive issue, one that I plan to avoid as much as possible.

The challenge to me is how to explain a grammatical structure in simple terms that the students can understand. This week's challenge will be to teach prepositions, never an easy task to explain. I've drawn about 20 pictures to show them visually what prepositions do. I hope they understand. Each class has a wide range of English speaking abilities. Some students speak almost no English and others are almost fluent.

Some of my "liberal" women students

Some of my men students

My Arabic tutor, Yayah, called me and we will resume classes two evenings a week starting tomorrow. Peace Corps doesn't have the funds at the moment to provide us tutors as promised so we are making our own contacts and exchanging English lessons for Arabic lessons. Yayah is a 20 year old Yemeni who lived in Somalia until the civil war drove his family out of the country. They first went to Saudi Arabia, but were kicked out of there after the Gulf War because they are Yemeni. Yayah had never visited Yemen until he came here a year ago. He is very homesick for Somalia. Two of his brothers and a little sister remained when the family left because there wasn't enough money for all of them to leave. The family members in Yemen are trying to earn the money to send for the ones still in Somalia. While I was in the States, Yayah's little sister died of worms. His dream is to be a translator one day. So he wants to practice his English conversation with me. My heart really goes out to this gracious young man who is so bright and kind and has had and continues to face so many obstacles.

Yesterday, nine of us volunteers went to Ma'rib and Baraquish in two land cruisers. We left at 7:30 am and returned at 7 pm. It was a great trip into the desert, again, a spectacular trip down twisting mountain roads. Our driver was a real cowboy. I held my breath on many of the hairpin turns wondering if we would make it.

We first visited the ruins of the ancient city of Baraquish that was deserted around 800 AD when the town's well went dry. Many of the mud and stone walls are still standing as well as sections of the wall that wind around the town. You can see the ruins from quite a distance. Tribes, not the government, rule this whole area. But government soldiers are everywhere at road blocks and tourist sites. While we were exploring the site, our driver gave the soldiers half our water bottles. We were annoyed but sympathized with the driver's position because the soldiers were heavily armed and driving a pick-up truck with a mounted machine gun. They wouldn't let us take their pictures. You have to be careful in this area because the Bedouins like to highjack cars. A member of the British embassy lost his land cruiser at gun point two weeks ago. That's why we hired a tour company to take us. It's the safest way even if it did cost 500 rials a piece.

Ruins of Baraquish 　　　　　　　*Armed boys at Baraquish*

We drove on to the ruins of the Old Ma'rib Dam after a picnic lunch. Two sluice gates still stand in the hot desert sand a long distance apart. I looked for traces of the Queen of Sheba and King Solomon but only my fantasy located their wooing ground. We climbed on the walls and played in the sand dunes.

Sluice gate of the Ma'rib dam

Ma'rib is the most famous archeological site in Yemen. It was once the capital of the kingdom of Saba, an important site for caravans on the ancient incense route to stop. Ma'rib was known throughout the ancient world from India to Rome. The dam was built in the 8th Century BC. It provided irrigation to 96 square kilometers of fields for centuries. It was finally destroyed by neglect in the 6th Century AD, long after incense trade had ended.

A short distance from the ruins of the dam stands the remains of five pillars of the Temple of the Moon. A sixth pillar is broken. Yemenis call this site the Throne of Bilqis. Bilqis is the legendary Queen of Saba, or as we know her, the Queen of Sheba.

Temple of the Moon

Our final stop was the Old City of Ma'rib. It was similar in many ways to the city of Baraquish that we had first visited but a little more intact. We were amazed to find people still living in some of the houses that had escaped with minimal damage caused by an earthquake in the 1970's and the bombing of the city during the civil war in the 1960's.

After buying his qat our driver began the three hour trip out of the hot desert back to the cool pleasant climate of Sana'a.

Until next time,

Baraquish

Eric's super human strength

Taxi Service

May 8, 1992

Greetings,

There are only three more weeks of school left. The midterm was skipped because of the very short semester! We have to make up and give a joint English exam to approximately 2000 students on June 7th. Four of us will have the pleasure of correcting the exams. It will take a good week of long hours to finish this chore I'm told. We should be finished with all our work between the 15th and 18th of June. Classes for the fall semester will not begin until sometime the end of September or the beginning of October. Nice long break! I can't believe how short the semesters are and how long the vacations are. I will have a project to spend time on. We have to put together a book for the more advanced English class next year. Probably this will mean photocopying pages from existing ESL books. Although, we are talking about creating our own material that is sensitive to Yemeni culture.

I think I've found my secondary project that we are all supposed to have. At a women's party a couple of weeks ago we met the manager of a women-in-development project. She is looking for volunteers to work with her. Basically, the volunteers work with poor women who are mostly refugees from Saudi Arabia, Somalia, and Sudan. They live in a camp constructed with discarded materials like cardboard boxes and corrugated tin for the roofs. The floors are dirt. There is no running water in the camp or a sewage system. Diseases run wild in the camp. The refugees are illiterate and don't have even a rudimentary understanding of health care and the need for sanitation to stop the spread of diseases.
The center where I will be working encourages women to come with their children and learn how to clean and care for them. They are also taught nutrition and disease prevention, and how to read and write. One of the center's primary goals is to teach them a handicraft skill so that they can earn some money

I will be working at the center one morning a week, to begin with, in the health care unit helping women bathe and care for the children. It is amazing what these women don't know about disease prevention and hygene. For example, when babies are just a couple of days old, mothers put vegetable oil in all their orifices. They even put their fingers down the baby's throat in order to stretch the opening so that the baby can scream better. If the baby dies, it is Allah's will. Infant mortality is high in Yemen. Many women die in childbirth, too. During the delivery, a midwife is present as a male doctor cannot see a naked woman. The woman delivers a baby under a blanket for modesty's sake. You can imagine the

The manager of the Woman's Center and her assistant

result if there are complications. I'm sure working at the Women's Center will be quite an experience for me. The Peace Corps women who will work there will be the first Americans to volunteer. There are a number of European and Indian women who are involved with this project. I just hope my stomach is strong enough to handle what is expected of me. You know what a coward I am when it comes to diseases and illness. I've always said I hope I am never in a situation where someone's life depends on my action. Maybe I'm about to be tested.

The women's party I went to was given by one of our former Arabic instructors, Eman. Just women are allowed at these parties because the women take off their veils and let their hair down. Underneath all that black they are quite fashionable in a polyester way. Most of the women were wearing bright flowery dresses, much makeup and a lot of gold jewelry. Eman and Silta, another one of our instructors, are stunning women. We had all we could do to control the gasps when we saw them in normal clothes. The TV was blaring with some Egyptian movie. We all sat in the mafraj drinking tea, eating cookies, and talking. Sometimes the women dance at these parties. This didn't happen this time. When we got ready to go, the Yemeni women slipped into Eman's bedroom and put on their long black robes and veils and went back out into the Sana'a streets as quiet black ghosts, showing only their big brown eyes.

Politically, things are getting hot here. Did you hear about the kidnapping of the Saudi ambassador? He was held hostage in his embassy for 18 hours. The tension between these two countries is obvious. A lot of the tension has to do with old border disputes; both countries claim land in the eastern part of the country, beyond and north of Ma'rib. This area is where oil has been found in Yemen. Now Saudi Arabia claims the land and has sent warning letters to the oil companies. Once before, Saudi annexed Yemeni land for which there is great resentment here. We hear that Saudi troups are more numerous at the border. In the YEMEN TIMES there was talk of war, but the Yemeni people I've talked to think that's just a journalistic exaggeration.

Yemen is the only country in the Gulf that is trying to become democratic. Elections are coming up that will decide if unification with the South of Yemen will be formalized. There are many political factions competing for power including the fundamentalist Arab Brotherhood. Supposedly the Saudi government is supplying money and guns to Bedouin tribes in the desert to disrupt the unification process. The Bedouins were loyal to the old emir who was deposed during the Yemen war of independence in the 1960's. Saudi Arabia tried to squelch the democratic process during that war, too. Iraq has sided with Yemen against Saudi Arabia during these conflicts. That is a big reason why Yemen supports Iraq and Saddam Hussein.

There was an attempted assassination of the minister of justice a couple of weeks ago. He was flown to Germany for medical treatment. This past week five men were gunned down in Tahrir Square, the Times square of Sana'a. There was an attempted bombing of the French embassy. Frequent demonstrations are held against UN sanctions of Lybia, mostly directed at the British, French, and American embassies.
Am I afraid? No! I have not detected any hostility from the people I see at the University or in the streets. We see pictures of Saddam everywhere because he is a hero here. People don't like the role of the US government and can't understand the loyalty to Saudi Arabia which is not a democracy, but they seem to be positive about Americans. To show you mainly why I'm not afraid, there was a massive demonstration against the UN sanctions that took place yesterday. The march was to go to the British, French and American embassies. They marched by the British and French embassies; on the way to the American embassy that is on the outskirts of Sana'a they passed a big qat suq. Most of the participants left the march to go buy qat and spend a quiet, mellow afternoon with friends. So much for political action.

I have a number of Palestinian students at the university as there is a large number of Palestinians living in exile in Yemen. I like them very much. President Bush is not a favorite person and they are frustrated about the lack of sensitivity and understanding Americans seem to show about their exile, but again I do not find them hostile. I am just careful about what I say when I'm asked a loaded question. I feel safer in Sana'a than I would in some parts of New York or Washington. I now carry my own green card. This card gives me more freedom of movement and respect because I'm working here and am not a tourist.

You may be wondering why I am so open about this political discussion. To date none of our letters coming to us or going to the US have been opened, just the packages. In fact some of the volunteers have their friends and families send them money in letters. The money arrives safely. It sometimes takes a long time for letters to arrive, but eventually they get to us.

I'm sure it's calmer here than in the Los Angles riots we have heard bits and pieces about. Unbelievable. Our Yemeni friends have been watching the riots on TV. They think the whole country is falling apart and that it must be dangerous to live in America. I can't wait to get my Newsweek and read about what happened in LA. Furthermore, our Peace Corps director is in close contact with the embassy, and if we are in any danger we will be taken out of the country. Our safety is carefully guarded. I guess if they would fly me home for a mild case of hemorrhoids, they will fly me out of here if it is unsafe for me to be here.

We have a new country director. Joe Moyer's term was up and he has returned to Putney, VT. Before he left we had a big qat chew at his villa. In addition the the PCV's (Peace Corps Volunteers) there were embassy officials and many Yemenis. I chewed a bag full of qat. My cheek looked like I had a major toothache. It's gross when you spit out the green pulp, sort of like a cow's cud. The new director is a woman, Cecila Hitte, It will be interesting to see how she does in this male dominated society. But she has lived in Yemen in the past and has a great affection for the country. One of the Peace Corps staff members had a Yemeni lunch for all of us to mark this administrative change. We sat on the floor in the hallway of his house and ate with our fingers out of the same dishes. His Vietnamese wife and daughters served us. His second wife and family live in Aden.

Yesterday, Artis (23 years old), one of my best Peace Corps buddies, and I went to the Old City, near the funduq where we stayed for our training to have lunch with a Yemeni family there who befriended Artis. We climbed up the narrow winding stairs to the fourth floor and were showed into the mafraj. Muhammad, Artis' friend, was a waiter at the funduq during our training. He visited with us as did his younger brothers and sisters. There must be at least nine children and the mother is expecting again. She cooked us a delicious lunch of rice, mixed vegetables in a soup, and fetta, a sweet dough with honey which was very good. The Yemni tea is very sweet, but very good. Again we ate from the same dishes, sitting crosslegged on the floor. I'm beginning to enjoy this custom.

Artist and me in Al-Hudayda

Four young men, English majors at the university, have adopted me. They have been coming to my room to visit me since I started teaching there. Their English is quite good, but they want to have coversations with native speakers and asked me if I could meet with them to have conversations. So I meet with them on Monday afternoons between classes. They bring me tea and old copies of USA Today and ask me to explain American idioms. I've started giving them my old Newsweeks. You'd think that I was giving them something very special. They're so appreciative of the time I spend with them. They ask me questions about America and life there. Of course they are full of romantic notions. They think it must be a perfect place where all people are free and treated equally. It pains me a little when I think of the racial, ethnic, and religious prejudice they would have to endure from some people at home.

Last week they invited me to go to a restaurant with them to have dinner. They asked me what I wanted to eat. I told them whatever they wanted to eat as long as it was Yemeni. So we went to a fresh fish market where they bought a BIG fish that came from Al-Hudayda. We took the fish to a little restaurant near the University where fish is cooked in the special way. They told me that it would be better if we brought our own fish as it would be fresher. The fish was cooked in a tub like stove with a very hot fire, fueled by gas; it was blackened fish. The waiter brought the fish, split in half and put it on newspapers on our table. The five of us picked the bones clean with our fingers. It was the best white fish I've ever eaten. We also ate a bread served in a pan with honey poured over it, and a large flat bread that was soft and light that we dipped into a hot sauce. Hot as in spicey. We drank tea. It was a wonderful meal. They were so attentive I felt like royalty. They call me teacher as a very respectful title, the way we call someone doctor. Of course, I was the only woman in the very busy restaurant. Yemeni women don't eat in restaurants unless there is a special room for them where they can eat in private with their families so they can unveil. Everyone was staring at me, and I felt as if I were on stage. But foreign women are considered the third sex here and therefore have more feedom of movement than Yemeni women. Also it helps that I am older. My four horsemen, as Artis named them, are only 20 years old. In the group there are two Muhammads, one Yassin, and one Abdul Basset. One of the Muhammads is a football (soccer) player, the other a chess player. Abdul Basset is a table tennis player, and Yassin's sport is chewing qat. None of them are from Sana'a. They just study here. I really enjoy talking to them. They were quite pleased that I enjoyed our eating adventure and told me that we will eat out again soon.

Yassin Al-Hemeary, me, Abdul Basset, Muhammad Jahaf, missing Muhammad Mokbel

Well, that's my news for the moment. The weather has taken a turn here. Finally we are getting rain. Every day around 5pm it rains very hard for about an hour. Sometimes it hails. Because there is no drainage system, the streets become lakes. The dirt streets become pools of mud. Very unpleasant if you need to be out and about. But Sana'a is greening up. The drought appears to be over, Insha'Allah.

I transplanted basil, parsley, dill, chives, and sweet william that I had started in pots to the rough soil of our garden this morning. I have my fingers crossed that they will survive with my tender loving care and Miracle-Gro.

Until next time,

May 23, 1992

Hi Everyone,

This is a fast letter as I have a chance to send it to the States in a couple of hours.

Today is a big holiday, Unification Day, second anniversary. This afternoon I'm going to a qat chew, given by some of our old students from training. I went to a chew on Thursday with some of our male students at the University. It was in the apartment of one of the boys. There were 10 twenty-year old men and Fran and I. Can you imagine twenty-year old students wanting to hang out with a couple of old ladies in the States? We had a good time. They fixed dinner for us, an egg and potato dish. Then they walked us home.

This is the last week of classes at the University. We are working on the exam for our 2000 students. We don't know exactly how many will take the exam as some students never register for classes. They just come to take the final exam. If they pass the exam, they pass the course. We have to run the tests off on an old mimeograph machine and assemble them ourselves. As you can imagine, this project is taking us a long time.

This summer I expect to be working on curriculum and helping with the training of the new volunteers who are expected in July.I will be working at the women's center twice a week once school has finished. It is a sad place. The poor women and children who come through the door make you want to cry. After my first time there I got fleas. I had to take all my bedding outside to air in the sun. We see lice, malnutrition and children with scars on their bodies where their mothers burned them to rid them of illness. We help the children to shower, give them vitamins and food, mainly carrots, milk and bananas. My job so far has been to find new clothes for the children in the donated pile. They are so thrilled to have new (to them) clean clothes. So what if the clothes don't match and are often not the right size. The sad condition of these children breaks my heart.

Last week an obviously sick mother came in with her two month old baby. The baby was dying of malnutrition because the mother could not nurse him and she was only giving him sugar water. I think the baby must be dead by now. If you want to include some money in your next letter, I'll see that it is used to buy clothes or medicine for these children. As I told you before, it is okay to send money through the mail. Just $5.00 will buy an outfit for a child.

Until next time,

June 8, 1992

Happy June Everyone,

Greetings the day after the BIG FINAL. Yesterday I was at the University from 7:30 to 3:30 helping with the final exam. My job was to run around between the three rooms I was assigned and answer student questions about the exam as the proctors, called invigilators, didn't speak much English. Technically, I wasn't supposed to monitor the tests that we gave in three different time slots. But the cheating was so obvious that I had to step in. They don't have the same attitude towards cheating as we do. True, many American students cheat, but they know it is wrong and go to elaborate means to hide it. Yemeni students are very open about cheating. Smart students try to help their friends. They write answers on their hands. One woman had the directions (north, south, etc.) drawn on the palm of her hand. We taught them the directions in English as one of our lessons. I took points off her test paper for cheating. She had a fit and talked to a Yemeni proctor. The proctor told me that she had just written the directions on her hand to help her remember them! Anyway, I am now knee deep in exam papers. I have corrected around 100 already, and it doesn't appear as if I've made a dent.

As I write this letter I hear the constant ba-a-a of the sacrificial lamb outside my window. A big religious holiday that commemorates the end of Ramadan called 'Id al-Fitr lasts for a few days; it begins on Wednesday. Most people who can afford it buy a lamb and keep it in the courtyards of their homes. They have it butchered for the celebration. By Islamic law, they give a portion of the meat to poor people and share the meat with friends and neighbors. I hope they don't kill it here! Meanwhile its constant noise is not making us sympathetic about its impending death. In fact, we have named it the little "Nick." Nick is a swear word in Arabic, the equivalent of our "F" word. So you cannot call someone "Nick" here if his name is Nicholas. There was a volunteer here a few years ago with that problem, so he had to change his name!

Mainly, other than go to the University, my fun has revolved around qat chews these past 10 days. I guess that's not unusual since I'm living in Yemen, and the main social event, daily or weekly, is going to a chew. The afternoon before my birthday I went to Yassin's brother's house (one of the four horsemen) for a chew. The brother was on vacation in Jordan. I sat in the mafraj with 10 young men from 3 o'clock to 8 o'clock. Chews start in the middle of the afternoon after lunch and end between 6 and 8 o'clock. I stayed with the men to watch the 7:30 news in English. It's a rare joy when I get to see this news program. Most Yemenis I know don't have televisions.

You just hang out, chew and discuss whatever you wish. We talked about literature, politics, Islam and food that afternoon. When you chew you get thirsty, so the host always provides Pepsi and water, sometimes tea. Really, it is a very relaxing afternoon. The art of conversation is very important. It's great to talk with a variety of people instead of watching some inane television show. These students like to talk and have a lot of interesting things to say. The qat makes you a little mellow so there are no long, annoying arguments, or drunken performances. Qat is not a mind altering drug. It makes you reflective. At least that's all I've felt so far, just peaceful with good thoughts. You're supposed to bring your own qat to a chew, but my young men are quite solicitous so they bought qat for me and wouldn't take any money for it. They came to my house to walk me to the chew and walked me home afterwards. Again, unrelated men and women don't chew together unless, of course, you are a foreign woman and therefore a member of the third sex.

This past weekend (June 4th and 5th) I chewed both days. On the 4th, Artis, Beth (housemate) and I went to Zarrah Talib's house for lunch and a chew. Zarrah is a radio personality in Sana'a and Yemen. Every Yemeni knows who she is. She also used to be an actress in Aden where she is originally from and where life for women is a little freer. She also lived abroad for several years. She is in one of Artis' English classes, and they have become friends.

The lunch was given in honor of Ahmed, her nephew, one of our students from training school. He is leaving for Russia soon for an extended business trip. Zarrah is not a typical Yemeni woman. She is divorced (in her 40's I'd guess) and quite plump. She makes her own gin, a habit from her life in England. She is open, loud and fun loving. Several Yemeni men were there, also very unusual in Yemen. She served us chicken, rice, salad, sauerkraut, okra, mixed vegetables, great fruit and nuts. We ate Yemeni style in the central hallway under the garish ribbons and tinsel that decorate her ceiling because her mafraj is too small to accommodate the 15 people who were there for lunch. Beth and I were the only women present besides Zarrah. After lunch we crowded into the mafraj and began the chew. This chew was more Western in that there was much laughing, bantering, and loud voices that filled the room. Probably the gin that was consumed before lunch had an effect, too. Zarrah disappeared for a long time. When she reappeared she had changed into a flowing, long red dress. She had put on make-up and let her long black hair down. She sang for us and played a tape of a song her father had written about her when she was a child. She certainly has stage presence and knows how to be center stage. I liked her as she is a warm, strong, fascinating character. I'm sure life in Yemen must seem very restrictive to her. She belongs in Greece or Italy.

That evening my four horsemen and a friend of theirs with a car came to pick me up, and we all went to the Yemen Hunt compound for ex-pats to see a production of "Charley's Aunt" put on by a local group of ex-pat actors. It was a lot of fun even though the show was very amateurish. My students had a great time and loved the play. They had never seen a live production! They didn't know what to expect as Western theatre is so outside their experience. When I first had encouraged them to go they were hesitant as they thought the tickets (100 riyals each, about $3.50) were very expensive. But, fortunately, they were very excited afterward. They were among only a handful of other Yemenis. Most of the people in the audience came from the ex-pat community, including the American Ambassador. As Muhammad said to me, "I feel as if I have left Yemen!" Anyway, it was a great thrill for me to expose them to their first live theatre.

Last month I took the same crew plus some of their friends to the British Council to see a video of *Othello*. They had studied the play all semester without seeing a production of it. I don't know why their English professors don't provide the services that are available here or encourage them to go to plays like "Charley's Aunt." It would be so helpful for improving their English skills to say nothing of the pure enjoyment.

Yahya, my Arabic tutor, has left me because he finally found a job as a translator in a small company. He had a devil of a time getting the job as all his papers regarding his school education as well as a certificate stating his English proficiency are in Somalia. He couldn't be hired without the proper proof of his credentials. He had no way of getting them as there is no mail going into or out of Somalia. No ministry here would give him the papers unless he took the courses. So I went to the British Council to see if they could help. They were great and were used to dealing with such problems. They gave him an English test and wrote a letter stating his proficiency and only charged 200 riyals. Yahya only had 100 riyals so I gave him the other 100 for his birthday which was on May 27th. He had his sister bake me a great cake for my birthday. It was the heaviest pound cake I've ever lifted, but it was great tasting and not too sweet. Just this week he received great news. His two brothers, his uncle and cousins got out of Somalia finally after two years of trying. They are expected to arrive in Yemen any day. Yahya is understandably very excited. Now that he has a job perhaps he can afford to marry his cousin who is coming with his brothers. His mother has already told him he will marry her. It's very common here to marry cousins. I'll miss seeing him regularly, but I hope he will stay in touch.

My geography students

Yahya

Friday was a gem of a day. Some of my geography students, who were in my English classes, asked me if I would like to go outside of Sana'a for a chew with them. I, of course, jumped on that one. So I met them at the University, and we started out in a battered pick-up truck. I sat in the front with Hamid, my student who was fortunate enough to have a truck. The others sat in the back of the truck. We drove to the twin cities of Kawkaban, on the mountain top, and Shibam, at the foot of the mountain. I have written about these cities before. We went there during training. But it was fun to go back again and drive up the mountain instead of walking up. The road was little better than a logging road. On the top we enjoyed the big view of the valley and the pre-Islamic buildings. Then we drove back to Sana'a to have lunch in a favorite restaurant of theirs. We shared salta. The cook was a student friend of theirs. He could take off the bottle caps of Pepsi bottles with his fingers. They would pop like Champaign bottles being opened. I was quite impressed, and, of course, he put on quite a performance for me. As usual there were no other women in the restaurant.

After lunch more students joined us (we were now 15) and we drove out to Wadi Dhahr to Khalid's house (one of the students). The beautiful old house, not far from the Palace on the Rock where the last Imam spent his summers, hasn't been lived in since his grandfather lived there. It obviously was the house of a wealthy person. We went to the fourth floor to his grandfather's old mafraj and chewed. It is still furnished as a mafraj. The windows look out on his old garden and a ridge of tan mountains that surround the wadi. So peaceful and inspiring. We chewed until 7:30 that evening. My students had never chewed with another American, much less a woman. During the late afternoon everyone became quiet and lost in his own thoughts. They always kid us that we will see America at this time. Well, I didn't, but I was a little overwhelmed with thoughts of home. I guess because of the season, I was remembering lilacs in bloom and the green, green grass. I wanted you all to be here with me, sharing this special moment as the sun set and the mountains still remained very vivid in the light sky. The call to prayer gently floated in the windows, "Allah is great, Allah is great." It was a great day.

Geography students on Kawkaban

Khalid in his family home

The chew at Khalid's house in Wadi Dhahr

Until next time,

June 29, 1992

Hi Everyone,

This morning at the Women's Center I was very touched by an eight year old boy. I went outside to give milk, carrots, bananas, and crackers to the children who were waiting with their mothers to come inside to be bathed. Just imagine how these children look: thin, very dirty clothes, barefoot, matted hair, flies crawling on their impassive faces. They were very polite when I gave them food; they didn't grab for it even though I could tell they were hungry. There was one boy by himself. The Center rule is that children must be accompanied by their mothers or a female relative. The boy just stared at me with hollow cheeks and sad, big eyes as I fed the other children. I decided that he was going to eat, too, even though he was not with his mother. He took the food quietly and ate quickly.

I told Noura, the Yemeni manager, what I had done, and she went to talk to him and find out why he had come to the center alone. His mother had been banished from the slum village by his grandfather in March because she was pregnant. His father was in jail, and had been there for three years. Terrik doesn't know where she is, and he is the brunt of name calling and laughter. He followed the other families to the Center because he had noticed that they sometimes came back wearing clean clothes. He told us this in a passive, quiet voice standing in front of the desk where we register families.

Noura verified his story with the Yemeni women who work at the center and live in the same slum. What can I say? Noura, Holly, another PCV, and I had all we could do not to cry. Fortunately, Noura has a very big heart, and she broke all the rules of the Center. She told him he can come alone every day, have a shower, and that we will give him food. We set about trying to put together the best outfit we could. The pants had to be rolled, the man sized belt cut, the shoes stuffed with tissues, and the sleeves of his two-sizes-too-big denim jacket rolled, but he looked great, like a real dude. When he left the Center Noura gave him five riyals to buy candy because she said Yemeni parents give their children at least five riyals a day to spend on candy. Terrik stole all our hearts.

Terrik and me

A Women Center's family

Many of the children who come to the Center have fleas and lice. They often have distended stomachs. Many of them have scars from burns their mothers gave them. Some of the mothers believe that burning a person where the pain is will make the child better. Last week a mother brought her four small children (all under six) to the Center with burn scars in the middle of their foreheads. But, like children the World over, they emerge from their showers smiling and proud of their new clothes. We can't give them new clothes every time they come because there aren't enough clothes. Some of the volunteers work with the children's hair, combing and braiding so that they are beautiful when they leave.

I am worried about Yahya because I haven't seen him for a week, and I'm afraid that his brothers and uncle's family were on the boats that came from Somalia with cholera and AIDS. At first, the Yemeni government wouldn't let them leave the ships. Many people were dying. Finally, with the UN intervention, they were allowed to get off the boats. The last time I spoke with Yahya he hadn't gotten any word about his family. I am worried he might have gotten bad news.

Two weeks ago I went to Ta'izz, Ibb, and Jibla for a couple of days with Artis. It was during another celebration, 'Id al-Adha, which comes roughly two months after 'Id al-Fitr. I'm not sure of the religious significance. But it is a big celebration. Everything in the country seems to be shut down. Many people return to their villages to visit their families which is customary. Everyone has an ancestral village, even if they were born in Sana'a. Because of the holiday, the buses were not running making it necessary for us to travel by taxi for the five hour trip to Ta'izz.

What an experience the taxi ride was. It was a station wagon with two bench seats in the back of the front seat. A man, his wife, and baby rode in front with the driver. Artis and I and two men were jammed into the middle seat. I was lucky because I sat next to the door as it would not have been appropriate for me to sit cheek to cheek with a Yemeni man. Because Artis is an African American he is often confused for a Yemeni man. In the third row there were two men, one woman with a baby and two small children, fourteen of us in all counting the driver who had lived in Texas for a year. We stopped a couple of hours out for ful and tea, and later we stopped for qat as some of the men wanted to chew.

We drove through some of the most spectacular scenery I've ever seen. The road curved out over steep cliffs, and we could look down the terraced mountains into distant valleys. At one point, going through Sumarra Pass before Ibb, it is 3000 meters high (around 9000 feet I think). We felt as if we were in an airplane we were so high. The babies began to scream, I suspect, because the change in altitude caused their ears to block. Their mothers didn't know what to do, and I wanted to lend the babies my fingers to suck on, but I didn't think their mothers would appreciate my offer! The driver was another cowboy who passed cars on curves; he even tried to do this going up a hill. Of course seat belts are unheard of, and it would be impossible to put in enough for everyone in the car because everyone is so jammed in. A taxi won't take off for its destination until it is filled with people, but the ride only cost 135 riyals a piece.

It was green, soothingly lovely green around Ibb, the farm belt for Yemen. This area receives more rain than the rest of the country. Ta'izz was hot! Unfortunately many of the shops in the suq in the old city and the National Museum where the last Iman lived before he died were closed because of the 'Id holiday. So we didn't really get to see Ta'izz as it normally is. We did walk around the city, the old and new parts, but I think once you've seen the Old City in Sana'a it takes a lot to impress you. Ta'izz is not as conservative as Sana'a is though, and we saw many women who were not wearing veils. There were even a couple of upscale hotels that sold drinks. Artis and I took advantage of this to surround a couple of gin and tonics each.

Our hotel was classified as a one sheet hotel, meaning that there was only one sheet on the bed, and probably the sheet was only changed once a week. Pretend pillows and blankets were also provided. As you can imagine, the bathroom, with an up-to-date smelly Turkish toilet, was down the hall. The shower didn't have hot water, but I couldn't have brought myself to step into the dirt coated bathtub anyway. Showers were put on hold until my return to Sana'a. The rooms only cost 90 riyals, however. We chewed qat with the hotel owner in the afternoon. Some of the best qat in Yemen comes from this region.

After Ta'izz we took a one hour taxi ride to Ibb. Ibb, a small city, has a spectacular setting. The new city where our one-sheet hotel was is not so interesting, but the old city on a high hill overlooking the new city is very interesting. The streets are narrow and wind in confusing patterns around the top of the hill. Some of the streets lead to great vistas of the green mountains and valleys which my hungry eyes drank in. I made the steep climb to the old city at 7am while Artis slept. Of course, I got lost as I forgot to leave my bread crumbs. Fortunately my Arabic is good enough so that I could ask directions from several different people to find my way back to New Ibb. I was afraid I would go down the wrong way and end up in another town! The people I spoke to were quite amused by the strange "Amerikey" wandering around lost in their village.

A view above Ibb

Ibb

From Ibb we took the short fifteen minute trip to Jibla. I loved this ancient small town with its famous mosque of Arwa, a 12th Century queen, who had the mosque built. Two small children (a brother and sister no more than eight and nine years old) double teamed us, showed us the town and demanded riyals at the conclusion

Al-Ashrafiya Mosque

Artis with our guides

of the tour, but the 20 riyals we gave them was worth it. They were good guides. I definitely want to return to this town to explore more. But we were low on riyals and had to return home to correct exams; so we returned to Sana'a by another taxi. This time Artis, another man, and I shared the way back seat. The springs were gone, and we both arrived back in Sana'a with backaches.

Exams are done. Now we are cross-checking other teachers' exams. I really don't know when we will be totally freed from the University. Classes were finished the 27th of May. It's almost July and all is not finished! Next week 25 more volunteers are expected to arrive and begin training. Most of them will be health volunteers, either nurses or administrators, who will advise the health ministry about setting up viable programs to educate Yemenis about health care. Many of the new volunteers are older, even older than I am! A retired principal is on his way and will join us at the University in the fall. It will be nice to see some volunteers more my age. We are thinking of throwing a house party and inviting only those over 45. Identification showing proof of age will be required!

Our Peace Corps nurse, the one who medevac'd me, has hepatitis B and has been sent back to Canada. So we are temporarily without a nurse's services. That means that we have to take a dhabar to the embassy and see the American doctor when we need shots or have a medical problem. Speaking of dhabars, have I ever explained this form of transportation to you? A dhabar is a minibus. Several of them drive around the city on set routes. You hail one if it is going to or near your destination and squeeze in with the other passengers. The usual ride is 4 riyals, which makes them cheaper than taxis. Now that I am working at the Women's Center, I use them because it is too far from my house to walk. Even when I use the dhabar I still walk about a mile and a half each way. The dhabars and the taxis are pretty banged up, obviously having seen better days.

Some of you have asked me if you could quote parts of my letters to other people. I reservedly say yes. I don't want you to stress the negative things I have written about or use what I say out of context if it makes Yemenis look lazy or unintelligent. Such is not the case! I want you to stress that I like Yemen and the people very much. They are, for the most part, friendly, kind, and honest. They work hard on their relationships, stressing that their families, tribes, and friends are more important than material wealth or fame. Where we often just give lip service to these values, they try to live their lives by them. For example, if the father of one of my students wants him to return home for some reason like a wedding or family party, my student goes no matter how it affects his classes. Of course there are Yemenis who break these values, are not honorable or honest. Finally, remember what I express in my letters is only one person's perspective. I have only seen a small part of this country in my short time here. As I meet more people and have more experiences, my views may change.

I need stamps. I had to borrow stamps to send these letters back to the States. I have to repay them. If people want to hear from me they must send stamps. I thank those of you who have generously sent some to me. Sorry to ask for this favor but such is the life of a Peace Corps Volunteer.

Bye for now,

July 16, 1992

Hi Everyone,

Great news. Finally last Saturday we were cleared from the University. I'm free for an indefinite period, probably until October. Elections will be occurring at that time so I might be free longer. NO ONE KNOWS. I'm just going to enjoy the free time and ask no questions. Thanks for your tax dollar support! I will continue to work at the Women's Center two days a week, Monday and Tuesday. Noura, the manager of the Women's Center, and I are going to go to the orphanage started by Mother Theresa. We both are considering volunteering there one day a week. I'm sure I'll see horrible things there as Mother Theresa's nuns work with the poorest of the poor. I don't know how well I'll do if there is a position for me. I'll see. The orphanage is supposed to be overcrowded and understaffed.

The poor children at the Center continue to touch my heart. I wrote you about Terrik. Well, since we've let him come without a mother or female relative we've had a parade of orphans. In most cases the mother is dead and the father has remarried and doesn't want his children with his first wife to live with him. As a result, the orphaned children are forced to live with an uncle or grandparent. Because there are so many families living in the same house, the unwanted children are overlooked. They come to us very dirty, sad and hungry.

Yesterday a little four year old boy with a large burn spot on his rear that hasn't healed came to the Center. He was so cute and happy after we bathed him, but unfortunately we couldn't find any pants to fit him. We ended up putting a pair of woman's underpants on him and tied a scrap of cloth around his waist to hold them up. These orphan children come to the center in family groups. Usually the oldest child, between six to ten years old, in the family is in charge of his younger brothers and sisters. On Monday, Noura is going to take the volunteers to the village we serve so that we can see where the refugees are forced to live.

Yahya finally came to see me. As I wrote last time, I have been worried that his brothers and uncle's family might have been on one of the refugee boats with cholera that came from Somalia. They were. Everyone arrived safely in Aden except for a small cousin who died. Also, the sister he lives with lost a child to illness recently. Yahya wants to bring this sister to meet me sometime soon. I suspect he lives in a very poor situation and doesn't want me to go to his home.

My new Arabic tutor is Khalid, a former student from practice school. He is a great person and a good teacher. He arrives at my house two nights a week with a written lesson plan. He is very patient with me when he quizzes me on my vocabulary words. I swear all my language learning cells are dead. It takes so much practice before I can remember new words. My speaking vocabulary is very basic, but now I'm pretty confident with survival Arabic. At least I can move about the city and shop in the suq without too much trouble. Khalid has asked me a lot of questions about the Peace Corps. One day I took him to the Peace Corps office so he could ask the Yemeni employees there his questions.

His family owns a children's clothing store in Sana'a, and his father travels abroad a couple of times a year to buy merchandise for his store. I suspect that they are better off than most Yemenis. He confessed to me the other day that his family doesn't know that he comes to tutor me. They have forbidden him to have anything to do with Peace Corps people because they think we are missionaries who are in Yemen to convert people. His father is suspicious because he can't understand why we would leave our rich country and come to work in Yemen for so little money unless we are missionaries. Khalid went to our practice school without his parents' knowledge. He wants me go with him and my camera and sunglasses (the tourist look) so that he can show me his home. He'll explain to his mother that I am an American tourist he is helping. His mother doesn't speak any English so it will be easy to fool her he says. His mother is not allowed to leave the house unless she is with her husband or he gives her permission to attend a women's party. Men do all the shopping for women. Usually the only women who are found in the suqs are the lower class women. I told Khalid that I don't want to be part of the deception that he proposes and that I feel bad that his family mistrusts the Peace Corps. He assured me that he will work on changing their views.

I realize that I neglected to tell you in my last letter what happened to Nick, the sacrificial lamb that was enclosed in my landlords' courtyard. He was butchered outside my window. I looked out and saw a pool of blood and quickly looked away. The local butcher came to do the deed. Poor Nick's head was pointed in the direction of Mecca and just before the butcher drew the knife across his neck he said "bismi'llah" (in the name of Allah). This must be said just before killing any animal. If a Muslim eats meat in a Christian house in a non-Muslim country he has to say "bismi'llah" before eating the meat as he will assume that the animal wasn't killed properly. As our landlords are well off, it was their religious obligation, we learned, to buy the lamb, have him here, and finally have him butchered. They had to give most of the meat away to their poorer neighbors. They didn't offer us any meat, but I don't think we could have eaten Nick anyway, even though his bleating was annoying. In Yemen, butchers and barbers must marry members of butcher and barber families, not by law but by custom. No one with any social standing would let his son or daughter marry into such families. I've asked why this is true and have been told that it is the custom.

Khalid

Men in the Old City of Sana'a

Last week 24 new Peace Corps Volunteers arrived. We went to meet them last Friday. It was nice to see many older people. Our group is so young. Also last week, two PCV's from Morocco arrived on our doorstep. I enjoyed wandering around Sana'a with them. They are exploring south Yemen now and should return to Sana'a tomorrow before going back to Morocco.

Yesterday two of the four horsemen came to our house to chew qat with me and to say good-bye for the summer. They both are going back to their villages, Muhammad Jafah to Hajja and Yassin to Ta'izz. Muhammad Mokbel will stay with his family in Sana'a. Abdul Basset has disappeared from the group that spends time with me.

All is well with me. Thanks to those of you who have sent me stamps.

Later,

Children in Sana'a

August 8, 1992

Greetings from Yemen,

So how's the weather at home? I have heard that so far it is damp and unseasonably mild. Here we have entered another rainy season. Most days are overcast and rain appears imminent, but it rarely rains. It's cool and pleasant, almost like early fall weather at home. In fact, the summer has been quite nice with none of the hot sultry days so common in New England in July, and we have no need for an air conditioner. However, if you leave the high plateau Sana'a is on and go south to Aden or to the Tihama it is beastly hot.

I trust you all got some frankincense and myrrh (laban and myrrh in Arabic) that my mother forwarded to you. You break the large pieces gently into pebble sized pieces. Then select which incense (bahor) you want to burn and put the incense directly onto the charcoal which is already red hot. A smell will be released. I thought you might enjoy having this around at Christmas time.

We hear by rumor and brief reports on the BBC and VOA (Voice of America) that things are heating up again in the Middle East. I just found out a few days ago that troops have been sent back to Kuwait. I've starting asking my Yemeni friends as well as other PCV's for news they've heard. It's hard to tell if something serious is about to happen or if the journalists are hungry for news to report. Our Peace Corps director is downplaying everything. Certainly Yemen is in no position to get involved with any action. It's having all it can do dealing with high unemployment, health issues, waves of immigrants from Somalia, and its upcoming elections that are creating unease and violence here. If an attempt is made on Saddam's life (as rumor has it, it is going to happen), I do fear for our tenure here as he is a hero to many people in Yemen. Time will tell.

My summer is progressing nicely, a lot of time to rest, study Arabic and read. I wander around Sana'a but haven't done any traveling outside the city lately. I plan to visit a nurse volunteer in early September in the mountains of northwest Yemen. It takes a whole day to travel there by bus, taxi, and finally local transportation up the mountain to her village. It should be quite an adventure. I don't dare look forward to it too much as my long anticipated trip to Sa'da never happened. The two Moroccan volunteers I mentioned in a previous letter invited me to go with them. The night before we were supposed to go, I had an attack of diarrhea and didn't dare make the four hour bus trip with them. Needless to say, buses are not equipped with bathroom facilities. In fact, I defy anyone to find a public restroom in Yemen. Oh for a good old gas station bathroom. I was sick for a couple of days. The women enjoyed their trip to Sa'da and Yemen. They have returned to the States to start graduate school. Liz is going to study at the Fletcher School at Tufts. She's an '85 graduate of Dartmouth. I enjoyed the two weeks Liz and Erin stayed with us.

While they were here, Christie, who works at the Yemen desk in Washington and who was very nice to me during my stay there in March, arrived in Yemen for six weeks. She is touring the country looking for new sites for the nurses who just arrived. She was a volunteer in Morocco with Liz and Erin and got to see them before they returned to the States. I made a marinara sauce and hosted a reunion meal for them. Christie will return to Washington at the end of August.

I mentioned in my last letter that we were going to visit Mahwa, the village where the families live who come to the Women's Center. Let me tell you, it was quite a shock to see where they actually live, even though I was prepared to be dismayed. The village covers a good acre. It is filled with tiny make-shift one room shacks made from any kind of available material, cardboard boxes and corrugated tin. Noura, the Center manager, led Holly, a PCV, a Swiss volunteer at the Center, and me through the village. Terrik recognized us and came running to see us. Holly took a picture of the two of us. He hasn't come to the Center the last few times I've been there. We don't know why because he certainly needs new clothes.

The wind roars through the narrow dirt streets scattering dust and enormous piles of litter. The narrow lanes are clogged with people. We passed a woman nursing her baby; another had her young son over her lap and was attempting to take the lice out of his hair. One man stopped us and wanted to know what we were doing in the village. He asked our nationality and didn't like the fact that Noura was showing Americans through the place as he had been kicked out of Saudi Arabia as a result of the Gulf War. He didn't want Americans to see how he was forced to live. He felt humiliated having his oppressor (in his mind) see him in such a state. We were a little nervous at that point and felt we should leave because our presence was intrusive. But Noura wanted us to continue. People stared at us from their dark doorways (no windows or electricity in the huts, also no running water). The Black refugees from Sudan or Somalia live in the poorest section as there is prejudice even here against them. One of the women who works at the Center lives in one of the best houses in the camp. It is made out of cinder blocks and has a couple of windows. She invited us in to have tea with her. Yes, I drank it with reservation, but I didn't want to insult the woman's generosity. Her mother, daughters, and grandchildren crowded into the room to stare at us. Visiting the village was a haunting experience that I will long remember.

The women and children come to the Center for showers and clean clothes; what they get is only a temporary bandage. They need to be provided decent housing with basic facilities, running water and proper sewage disposal. The children return from the Center clean and go back into filth and disease. It seems rather hopeless what we do. They only find temporary respite at the Center. Over a thousand people live in Mahwa, the refugee village. There are other programs provided at the Center in addition to what we do. Health education, sewing, basket weaving, and literacy classes are the main ones offered. A group of women is always weaving baskets at the Center when I am there. Last Tuesday I spent most of my time watching them and trying to talk to them as we were not busy looking after children.

Basket weavers at the Women's Center

My friends Arlene and Sally sent me some money to buy things for the children. I bought several pairs of pants (like sweat pants) from a peddler on the street. It gave me a lot of pleasure to give those clothes to children as I felt that Sally and Arlene were with me, and I know they would have felt good to see the children leave proudly wearing the clothes.

I have met some interesting ex-pat women who volunteer at the Center. One of the women is a Syrian doctor who works for a British group. She is mainly working with cholera cases. I had lunch with her and her husband and two children last week. We sat in chairs around a kitchen table – a real treat. They are an interesting family. She told me I could go with her when she travels to Hajja in September when she goes to treat people in some of the villages. I am looking forward to that. But, like everything else about my life here, I'll believe it when it happens or as the Yemenis say, inshallah (if Allah wills it). Another woman who just started volunteering is a Swiss nurse. Her husband is an American who teaches at the International School. I haven't met him yet as he is visiting his family in the States. Today I had lunch at a Yemeni restaurant with her and her two children.

The health problem in Yemen is enormous, especially in the villages that are often difficult to get to in this mountainous country. The problems have grown because of the million refugees who came back from Saudi Arabia after the Gulf War. Seeing what I have seen takes the starch out of the Star War extravaganza that was the Gulf War for those of us who watched it on CNN in the clean, well-lighted comfort of our living rooms. I wish President Bush had to walk through Mahwa. Wars sometimes solve some problems, but they create others. Because of the civil war raging in Somalia, thousands of refugees are pouring into Yemen. They are mostly coming in through Aden and are being detained in camps there. At an ex-pat party a couple of weeks ago I talked with a man newly arrived at the US Embassy. He had accompanied an American official who came to Yemen to investigate the problem of dealing with the huge number of refugees. He said the situation is appalling. There is little food or medicine for these people. How can a poor country like Yemen deal with such a massive influx of refugees? Yemen is the only county in the Gulf that will take these refugees. So much for oil rich Saudi Arabia. I am beginning to share the Yemeni attitude toward that country. Fortunately the UN is involved now. I wonder about the spread of disease. All I know is that I gladly offer my body when the nurse wants to give me a shot for some heretofore disease unknown to me.

I went with Noura to visit the Mother Theresa Home to see if we could volunteer to work there. The nuns told us that there is no work that we could do because it would be dangerous to work there as the patients are all mental patients, either mentally challenged or insane. Some of the inmates are chained they said. We would have to have special training to work with them. NO THANK YOU!! I don't know how the nuns can do the admirable work that they do.

I am enjoying great fruit this summer. It's grape season, and the grapes are the best I've ever eaten, even after they are washed in water with some bleach. What a shame that they don't enjoy wine here. Next year I will try to make some wine. Please send me any wine making recipes you may have. I have also been enjoying mangos, papayas, raisins and prickly pears. Bananas are always available. The melons, cantaloupe and honeydew, are huge and wonderful. I ate my first pomegranate a couple of weeks ago. UGH. Hundreds of tasteless seeds inside a tough skin. I really don't know why Persephone was tempted to indulge.

I am still enjoying Khalid, my Arabic tutor. He is such a kind young man and has taken it as his responsibility to look after us. He stopped by the other day to tell us we should not be on the streets after 9pm. There have been a number of shootings at night, and although the violence isn't directed at us, he is afraid we might get caught in crossfire. Sounds like any city at home. Our phone suddenly went dead, and as our landlords are on vacation in Egypt, Khalid went to the phone company to report our problem. He found out that our phone had been turned off because we hadn't paid the phone bill that HASN'T BEEN ISSUED YET! Another example of Yemeni logic. But the phone is working at the moment.

Kahlid came by and showed us how to make ful and ate with us a few days ago. Peace Corps is finally going to come through with money for Arabic tutors so I can pay him. I have also hired Noura, who resigned as the Women's Center Manager, to give me lessons twice a week. All together I'll study with a tutor five hours a week. I don't know if I'll make great progress. But I'm trying.

Yahya comes to visit about once a week. He often brings two of his friends with him. On Saturday mornings I am going to speak English with them for an hour because they want to practice speaking. Yahya's family is reunited now; his parents, brothers, sisters, uncle, and cousins are living in a house in Sana'a. I hope I get to meet them one day. Beth's brother Andy is visiting us from the States for a couple of weeks. So we're catching up on US news. Unfortunately he is a Cleveland Indians fan so he doesn't have Red Sox news for me.

Walking is keeping me in good shape. I would love a nice piece of ham. Because it is forbidden here, I guess that's why I miss it. Thanks for your letters and stamps. It's always wonderful to hear from home. Sounds like Clinton has a shot. YEA! Red Sox? Olympics?

Until next time,

August 28, 1992

Hello from Yemen,

Did I say something about rain threatening but never materializing in my last letter? Well, let me tell you I stand corrected! We have had a lot of rain this August. Buckets of the stuff have fallen all over Yemen. Actually it is a good thing for the country as the crops should be good and the drought is over. My little herbs are dancing with joy because of the rain, and I've cut some parsley and chives to put in a salad. I don't know how much longer the rains will last, but I am selfishly getting sick of them. Each day begins in sunshine and ends in showers. All my shoes are caked with mud.

As you can imagine, the rain is causing problems in Mahwa (where the people who are served by the Women's Center live). Of course their roofs leak, soaking everything and turning their dirt floors into mud. They must spend a lot of time trying to bail out their houses and dry everything out while the sun shines. Therefore, not many of them have been coming with their children to the Center.

When I go to the Center I spend most of my time trying to talk with the Mahwa women who work at the Center and are leaning how to weave baskets. One older woman, Mama Josah she's called, is teaching the group of women to make the baskets so that they can earn some money and won't have to beg in the streets. Her daughter Afrah is her assistant. I enjoy TRYING to speak Arabic with them. They teach me new words, correct my pronunciation and share tea and bread with me. It is an incredible opportunity for me to sit with these women and share some human warmth and understanding. I think they have grown as fond of me as I have of them.

Yesterday when I arrived, Afrah came outside to greet me and walk me inside holding my hand. In Yemen, friends, men with men and women with women, hold hands when they walk together. Mama Josah invited me to go to her house for lunch, but I unfortunately had plans and couldn't go. She told me that someday I would have to go to her house to smoke the mada'a and chew qat. That should be an experience if it happens. I bought four baskets that Mama Josah made. They will always be special to me because I sat with her and watched her make the baskets. A basket takes three to five days to make. They sell each basket for 200 to 300 riyals ($8 to $9).

Mama Joesah and me at the Women's Center

Basket Weavers and me

A couple of Fridays ago, Artis and I went to Zahrah's for lunch. A male friend of hers from the radio station where she works was also there. As I've said before, Zahrah is not a typical Yemeni woman. Abdullah was soon in hot pursuit of me, trying to get me to cuddle up to him on the mufraj and grabbing at me. He told me I could take his car and drive it. He wouldn't accept the fact that Peace Corps forbids us to drive here, and he kept asking me if I would go to the Sheridan Hotel with him. Understand that he's married and has seven children. He even asked me to marry him. I'd be wife number two. I wanted to say, "Stop it you're a married man with children," but he wouldn't have understood my comment. After all, he's entitled to have three more wives if he can support them equally. He found my name hard to pronounce so he gave me the nickname "Tegeega".

After successfully fighting him off most of the afternoon we all piled into his car (I managed to find a safe place in the back seat), and he drove us into the mountains to visit Kawkaban (I had been there twice before), about 30 miles outside Sana'a. By the time we got there it started to get dark and began to rain. So we just started back toward Sana'a. But I just knew it wasn't going to be easy.

We've been taught to check out the condition of the tires before we get into cars as the cars are poorly maintained and often have bald tires. Most taxis have glowing oil lights, and the transmission sounds as if it will go at any minute. But I never thought to check out the windshield wipers. The one on the driver's side was just a stub with an old cloth wrapped around it. It certainly wasn't very effective. The rain beat down on the car as we began the trip back down out of the mountains on a road with narrow hairpin curves. Abdullah could hardly see and had to drive with his window down and head stuck out. When the lights from oncoming cars blinded him, he had to stop. At one point we drove through a stream flooding the road, and the water flew into the back seat, right into my startled mouth. I just knew he was going to drive us right over a steep cliff into eternity.

After what seemed like hours, we made it back to the outskirts of Sana'a where the rain had stopped. But our adventure wasn't over. He turned down an unfamiliar street in the opposite direction of downtown. The street was dark and filled with big trailer trucks. As we drove down the street on some secret mission I had my suspicion and felt like we were driving around Chicago during prohibition. I guess this suspicion was the result of too many movies set in that era because I wasn't born yet and have never been in Chicago. Sure enough, my suspicions were confirmed. We drove off the road and stopped to talk to a Yemeni man. He got in the back seat with us (we were now four in back). We resumed our journey down the dark street for another half mile or so. The man got out of the car and disappeared into a tall building for several minutes. During this time Artis and I were told nothing, and we didn't ask any questions. Finally, he returned to the car and gave Zade, Zahrah's boyfriend, a package. We drove the mysterious man back to his pickup place and then drove back to Sana'a. I turned my head to see what Zade had. It was a big bottle of American whiskey. So now I've had an experience meeting a Yemeni bootlegger.

I spent an interesting time in the suq in the old city recently. One evening I went with Cecilia Hitte, the Peace Corps Director, to meet her friend who has a small (7 x 5) shop in the traditional medicine suq. Teriq is a charming man full of stories and good humor. Cecilia has known him for years. We sat on benches in front of his shop door like a big window that he crawls in and out of. At night he just shuts the shutters to lock his shop. Many of the shops in the suq are like that. He got us tea, and we visited with him for an hour. Cecilia took me because I was trying to find out what frankincense and myrrh looked like so I could buy some. There are all kinds of incense in Yemen with all kinds of smells. But I wanted to find some pure frankincense and myrrh which are not popular with Yemenis. They like the more perfumed versions of incense. Teriq showed me both and showed me how to tell the difference between the two. I bought some of each from him at a good price. Frankincense is used now for medicinal purposes he said. You boil it in water and then drink it to relieve a sore throat. From several rows of tiny wooden draws he extracted rocks and herbs and told us how to cure ailments from rheumatism to AIDS to impotence. I have since been back twice with other people. We are all fascinated with his stories and medical cures.

Teriq's pharmacy

Noura and I went to an International Women's meeting at the Taj Sheba Hotel one rainy morning a week ago. We met an American woman, newly arrived with her two young sons, a Scottish woman and a Dutch lady. We decided to explore the old city together with Noura as our guide. She took us to a traditional old family house with three generations living in it. Her sister is married to one of the sons and lives in the house with her husband and children. They were very nice about letting us tour the house, even allowing us to go onto the roof to take pictures of the city. We later had tea with the resident old lady who was quite weak having just recently been released from the hospital. As we continued to wander through the old city, Noura's seven year old nephew, Muhammad, tried to extend friendship toward the two American boys with us. Stephen, the seven-year-old had a hard time holding hands with Muhammad, but Craig, the ten-year-old, was a real good sport and walked around the old city hand-in-hand with Muhammad.

Khalid took me to visit his father's store on Gamal St. one evening recently. This is the same father who doesn't want Khalid to have anything to do with Peace Corps people. Khalid instructed me not to mention Peace Corps. I was to say that I was a teacher at the University and that I'd met Khalid while I taught at NIAS where we had our practice school. Since I didn't have to lie to his father I agreed to do as he asked. The store is tiny, about 10 feet by 20 feet, and stuffed with Western style baby's and small children's clothes. I sat on a small stool and drank tea, conversing with Khalid's father for an hour. His English is exceptional, and his direct astute mind made him an interesting person to talk with. We covered the usual topics: politics, the Middle East problems, World economic woes, and the beauty of Yemen. I enjoyed talking with him very much. Khalid said that I passed his father's test with flying colors. I was just so nervous that I would blow Khalid's cover, and I did feel dishonest about not mentioning the Peace Corps or that Khalid is my Arabic tutor.

As most of you are aware, things are heating up a bit here. There is first of all the worry about Saddam Hussein and what will happen in Iraq. The Yemenis feel very strongly that the West should stay out of the situation. The Yemen government has come out in favor of Iraq. Who knows how Saddam will retaliate for the American and British planes flying over the south of Iraq. I guess it will be a waiting game until he takes some action. Secondly, as the October election draws closer here, the violence appears to be growing. Last week a missile was launched at the president of the parliament's house. It landed in his bedroom. Fortunately, he and his family were not at home. He is a member of the socialist party. Twenty-five socialist party members have been killed or attempts have been made to kill them in recent months. The socialists are from the south. The socialist vice president has returned to Aden with his private army of 1000 men as he fears for his life in Sana'a. Some Yemenis fear that he may try to raise an army and civil war will erupt. A letter has been sent to Ali Abdullah Salah, the President of Yemen, who has a private army of 70,000 men I'm told, demanding that he investigate the murders and attempted murders of the socialists. Some people believe that President Salah ordered the murders because he fears the socialist strength and doesn't want to lose the election. Some Yemenis say that if he does lose he won't step down. There are two police groups competing for power in Sana'a. One group is charged with the safety of Sana'a. The other group is supposed to take charge in case of war. The opposing police groups have had a couple of shootouts recently, one in the center of Sana'a where seven people were killed, the other quite near the Peace Corps office where three people were killed. Khalid told me that Yemenis are beginning to stock up on food supplies in case there are problems. He said his father has bought a gun to keep in the house. I'm surprised he didn't have a gun as this society is armed with machine guns. The American Embassy officials and Peace Corps officials are downplaying the problems swirling about in this part of the World and don't think there is reason for concern, just caution. I'm not sure what the true story is. I try to listen to VOA or the BBC every day. The next couple of months should be interesting to say the least.

One of the volunteers is house sitting for an American Embassy official this summer. She recently had three of us over for lunch. I was overcome when I walked into the well-furnished villa. Plush Western style furniture, beautiful carpets, real beds, a normal dining room with table and chairs and a kitchen filled with gadgets: a real stove, a microwave, and a blender! Most of all, I was overwhelmed by the stereo and disc player. Lisa let me pick out a CD to play. I selected one of Mahler's symphonies. Listening to such beautiful music on top-of-the-line equipment made me almost cry. Being in that house reminded me of all the things I am missing at home, but I still feel so fortunate to be able to have the adventure I am having.
I broke a filling and had to go to an Egyptian dentist. I dreaded it, but Peace Corps found a passable one for me. As far as I can tell, he did a good job. The only thing I didn't like was that he only wore a rubber glove on one hand, the one he didn't put in my mouth!

So that's all for this month folks. I hope in my next letter I can tell you about my adventures in Afla Hasham, a mountain village in the northwest where Jolene is a midwife volunteer. To those of you about to start school, READ MY LIPS. No school for me until October!

Until then,

Volunteers relaxing

Another view of the Old City of Sana'a

September 7, 1992

Dear Friends and Family,

Saturday I returned from the most incredible trip to Afla Hasham, a mountainous area in northwest Yemen (I'm not sure of the spelling because I couldn't find it written in the Latin alphabet). Jolene, a nurse volunteer who joined Peace Corps when I did, and Bill, a lab tech volunteer who had just completed his tour, were assigned there. Three of us, Eric, Lisa, and I, had been planning a trip there since the beginning of the summer. We almost waited too long because a few days before we were supposed to go Jolene came off the mountain to resign from Peace Corps. She had had enough of the isolation she faced daily in the mountain village and the tension that is countrywide because of the pending November election. So far we have lost four out of the original sixteen in our group. Four of the new trainees have also resigned. Anyway, the three of us got to go back to Afla Hasham with Jolene and help her pack up her things. Actually, it was easier for us to travel there than it had been for most people who visited because a Peace Corps driver drove us there in a land rover and another driver followed us with a truck.

We left Sana'a at 8:30 Thursday morning, September 3rd. The three hour trip to Hajja was pleasant and the mountain scenery spectacular. The road was winding, but nevertheless it was paved and smooth. We stopped for lunch in Hajja and shared some salta. It's difficult to find much else for lunch other than salta or rice with over cooked vegetables. After we left Hajja our journey began in earnest. For about two hours we drove on a bumpy dirt road down into the Tihama, the desert that follows the coast of Yemen. It got very hot, and the dust beat into our faces because we drove with the windows open.

Finally we reached a paved road and headed north through the Tihama to Abs. In Abs we turned east to head into the mountains again. But first we had to drive for almost two hours through a wadi, a dry river bed that becomes a rushing river when it rains. The wadi was wide and sandy. The road was just tire tracks left from vehicles that had preceded us since the last rain. It was like riding on a bumpy beach minus the ocean. But let me tell you, the scenery was amazing. Grass huts you imagine you would find in Africa, camels, goats, sheep, donkeys, people on motorcycles, birds, little villages, trucks carrying supplies, shrubs, huge cacti, girls and women pulling water from wells and then putting the containers on donkeys to begin the long trip up mountains (an all-day process for them), sand swirling, sand in your face, sand in your mouth, brown, brown World.

Typical Tihama house

Redman letting air out of the tires to drive in sand

At 4:30PM we reached the base of the mountain that led to Jolene's little village in Afla Hasham. It soon became very apparent why a four-wheel-drive vehicle is necessary to go up the mountain. There is no road, although they call the narrow, mountain hugging, incredibly steep, rocky path "a road". Sometimes only a couple of feet existed between our vehicle and space that drifted down into deep ravines and valleys. Now you don't really think there were guardrails do you? From my place of honor in the front seat I took some pictures and was pretty mellow about the hour and a half trip up the mountain because we had bought qat in Abs and were all pretty laid back by this time, even Redman our driver.

The little stone villages perched on distant mountain peaks, the frequent donkeys loaded with bags of supplies or water containers, women carrying incredible loads of water or vegetables on their heads, children or women herding goats, and green terraces rimmed with stone walls was a Disney World scene. It wasn't real; I wasn't really having this adventure. But the clutter, plastic bottles and plastic bags tossed aside by Yemeni travelers up the mountain made me realize it was real, not pristine clean Disney World. Finally we arrived in the tiny village around six pm, just in time to witness a hazy sunset. While Jolene informed Bill about their move from the village the next day and told the doctor that she was leaving. Lisa, Eric and I walked around the mountain top. We drank in the amazing panoramas of mountain peaks, deep valleys, terraces, mountain people, and stone houses. Very few Westerners have ever visited this place. Jolene and Bill were the first Peace Corps people stationed there. The elevation is lower than Sana'a's between 4000 and 5000 feet so we had to take malaria pills because the malaria carrying mosquitoes are found below 5000 feet.

View from Afla Hasham

Eric & Lisa

Road up Afla Hasham

Girl carrying water

The next morning we got up at 5:30. Eric, Lisa and I climbed to the top of a mountain peak above the village. We met many children out walking, playing, or beginning their trip down the mountain to get water. Jolene finished packing during this time. We had helped her do most of it the night before. Then after a quick breakfast we loaded the truck and land rover with Bill's and Jolene's things. The villagers came to watch the process. Some of them came into the house and started going through some of her things. Her landlord started pulling up some of her corn. He said he did that to thin it out so it would grow better!

At 10am we began the trip down the mountain. It was as spectacular as the trip up the mountain. This time when we reached Abs we continued south through the Tihama to Al-Hudayda. We arrived at the Bourg hotel at 3:30. Eric, Lisa and I registered, and the rest of our party continued on to Sana'a.
We caught a dhabar that took us way out beyond the town to a private little area on the Red Sea so that we could swim in private. Our swim was refreshing even though the water was very warm. The sunset was not that great because it was cloudy. We had to hitch a ride back into town. A couple picked us up. She was driving fully veiled, but as it turned out her husband was giving her a driving lesson. She was BAD! First she took off before Eric was all the way in the car, and he had to hop along until we got her to stop. Then she and her husband, who was doing the steering, kept turning around to talk to us. The car would head for the rock wall, then into the on-coming lane. We were very glad to leave that car!

In a little restaurant near the hotel we ate blackened fish. The next day I sat on the covered balcony and read, enjoying the view of the Red Sea and Al-Hudayda while Lisa and Eric went swimming. It was very, very hot. We left by bus at 2pm to go back to Sana'a. It was a long five-hour trip, but again the scenery was beautiful as we again climbed up to the plateau and the cool pleasant weather of Sana'a.

Muhammad Jafah called me to invite me to visit him and his family in Hajja this coming weekend. What a great opportunity. I have visited and eaten in Yemeni homes, but I have never stayed overnight. Again, another adventure. I am just nervous about what I'll do about drinking water. I think I'll put a bottle of water in my luggage. I bet they don't boil water or drink mineral water in his home. I will be very careful in Hajja because there is cholera in the area as well as malaria carrying mosquitoes. Khalid centered his lesson this evening on the proper greetings I should use and how I should act in Muhammad's home. I will also have to bring my own toilet paper because Yemeni's don't use it.

That's all for now everyone,

Old City buildings connected   *Typical dukan*

Yassin, me, Muhammad Mokbel with Yassin's nephew and nieces

September 21, 1992

Hi Everyone,

As I wrote last time, I was invited to visit Muhammad Jafah, in Hajja. On September 10th Holly, another PCV, and I left from Sana'a by taxi at 8:30 am. Taxis are VERY crowded so we decided to pay for an extra seat so that our ride would be more comfortable, and it was, as we had the way back seat, which is supposed to be for three people, to ourselves. The taxi that departed just before us had a sheep in the storage area, like a trunk for luggage. That must have been a fun ride for the passengers! The trip took three hours through some spectacular mountain scenery. I had traveled this road the week before on my way to Afla Hasham. Muhammad and his friend Muhammad met us at the taxi station in Hajja.

As Muhammad's parents were doing repairs on their house, we stayed with his sister and her husband, who also is her cousin. Her mother-in-law lives in the same house with them along with their five children. It is forbidden to say the name of a woman to men outside the family in a fundamentalist Muslim family. To respect that rule I will refer to her as Muhammad's sister. His sister fixed us a delicious lunch of salta, bint-al-asha (a cake like dish served with a lot of honey over it), rice, shafot, and tea, but she couldn't eat with us or be in the same room because Muhammad's friend ate with us, and he was not a member of the family. The mother-in-law was hidden away in her room, also. We didn't even meet Muhammad's sister until I asked Muhammad if we could see her as I wanted to thank her for the lunch. He took Holly and me to a cook house outside the main house. She was working in the kitchen fully veiled.

After lunch, Muhammad and his friend drove us around Hajja. We visited the university branch where Muhammad's friend (known as Muhammad II hereafter) studies English. It's a nice small campus, like a community college, with breathtaking views of the lush, green mountains and rolling hills. We drove to the castle remains of ancient origin on top of the highest peak in Hajja.

Muhammad took us to his house to meet his mother, sisters and small brothers. Muhammad II couldn't come into the house with us. Then the neighbors, and aunts and cousins wanted to meet us so Muhammad had to leave the house so that they could come in. We smiled and nodded with them for about an hour before Muhammad called to us from the outside telling us that it was time to go. How strange that the men and women are kept so much apart, even more conservative than Sana'a.

Muhammad on left with his friends in Hajja

The Muhammads took us to a plush hotel in Hajja for afternoon tea. Muhammad II's uncle owns the hotel. Naturally the view was amazing, but then all the views in this picturesque city are.

In the early evening we went back to Muhammad's sister's house for a light supper of ful and tea. Ful is made with beans, chilis, tomatoes, onions, and coriander.

Muhammad II told Holly and me that he was divorced and that he has two children. On his wedding night he saw his bride for the first time and didn't like what he saw. So, after two children, he divorced her. Next time he gets married, he said, he's going to demand to see the bride first so that he will be able to see what he's getting!

Finally Muhammad II left about 9:30 so the sister could come into the mufraj and talk with us. Her husband Ibrahim wanted to know if we wanted a DRINK. Holly and I couldn't believe what he was asking us. He said, "If you want beer, whiskey, or gin I have it." We never expected to find alcohol served in this conservative house. I said I'd love a cold beer. I was promptly served a cold shot of gin. Ibrahim doesn't know what different kinds of alcohol are called. I was glad to learn that Muhammad doesn't drink because he is a very serious Muslim.

They brought mats, sheets, and blankets to us, and we slept in the mufraj that night. We were smart to bring our own toilet paper as there was none in the house that we could see. We had also anticipated an associated problem. Toilet paper will not flush down most Turkish toilets here; neither will anything else of any substance that you sometimes have to help along with a stick. We had brought individual plastic bags with us so that we could deposit our used TP in them and then carry back to Sana'a for disposal! Other than having to endure an attack of mosquitoes I had a pleasant sleep.

Hajja

The next morning we met the mother-in-law and talked with the children. When the two month old baby girl was left in the mufraj with us I wanted to unwrap the tightly wound cloths that restricted her movement so that she could kick her legs and flail her arms about. She looked so hot and confined. It was interesting to note that the family didn't appear to pay much attention to her. Her mother fed her, pulling out her breast with no modesty in front of us, Muhammad, her other children and her mother-in-law. Yet she can't show her face to a man not in her family. She didn't spend much time cooing and holding her baby as American mothers do with their infants. Her affection appeared to be directed toward her older children with whom she was very affectionate. In fact no one seemed to pay much attention to the baby. I'm not sure why this was the case. Because she was a girl? Yet the two older girls were treated with much affection. Perhaps, and this is pure speculation on my part, because infant mortality is so high here families don't invest much emotional attachment until the child appears to be a survivor. An interesting thing to observe in this family was that the older children showed no jealousy of the baby as American children often do of their baby siblings. I especially noticed that the two-year-old girl was seemingly indifferent to her baby sister. She was very secure with her mother, father, and older siblings. Muhammad and Ibrahim rented a four-wheel drive taxi to take us across the mountains to their ancestral village, Mayben. The four-wheel drive was necessary because the road was as bad as the one to Afla Hasham that I had traveled the week before. Along the way we stopped to have a picnic breakfast in a farmer's field.

Breakfast with Holly, Ibrahim, Muhammad and taxi driver

We ate yogurt, bread, meat, bisbas (chili) and juice. It was a pleasant setting. Many women and children walked by us carrying loads of things on their heads or driving sheep or cattle. When we left, the men folded our picnic blanket and left our trash behind. Holly and I wanted to pick up the trash as we couldn't believe that we were going to leave all that trash in a farmer's field. But we had to shut our American mouths so as not to insult our hosts. It's their country, but they treat it as one big dump. I hope that one day they will learn not to throw their trash carelessly aside. We laugh at ourselves as we walk the streets of Sana'a, empty gum wrappers in hand, looking for trash barrels that don't exist. The streets all over Yemen are littered by refuge. How powerful societal conditioning is.

Along the way to Mayben, we stopped frequently so that we could admire the spectacular mountain and valley views. At one point, we stopped on a plateau and sat with our feet hanging over the edge of the cliff and looked down into a steep valley. On the slopping mountain side, women watched grazing goats. A family of young girls on top of the plateau watched their goats graze. Ibrahim asked them for some fresh milk because I foolishly said I had never drunk goats' milk. When he offered us the bottle of fresh milk to drink, Holly refused to try it. I knew I had to drink some. I just let a little of the tangy substance pass my lips. On the outskirts of Mayben, we met a truck of cousins beginning their trip to Al-Hudayda where they go daily to sell the qat they grow. Ibrahim and Muhammad bought some qat from them for our afternoon chew.

Once in the village Muhammad took us on a walking tour of the place. Most of the people who live there are his relatives. He showed us the house where Imam Muhammad al-Badr lived before he escaped to Saudi Arabia, not far away, during the 1960's revolution. Northern Yemen was a Zabid strong hold for the imam and the royalists. Muhammad is a Zabid and his family is descended from the Prophet's family. They are considered among the most important families in Yemen. During the revolution, the republicans bombed this village extensively because the imam was there. Muhammad's family home was destroyed by bombs. Just the outline in a pile of rubble remains. During the bombing, many of the inhabitants left to hide in caves. Ibrahim told us that he knew of a secret tunnel leading from the village that can be used in time of war. That information is passed on from generation to generation because these people live with the expectation of war.

We went to a cousin's house for lunch. We never saw the woman who cooked it. The cousin is a teacher in the village. He wore a pistol tucked into his jambiya belt. The house had no electricity. The outhouse was a little shack outside as primitive as I've ever seen. Before we ate, the cousin came with a pail of water which we dunked our right hands into to clean(?) before touching the food.

Holly playing chess with the host

Muhammad and me

After Lunch, we chewed qat. Our host was called away to a big family meeting. Ibrahim went, too. One of the cousins had been in a car accident on his qat run to Al-Hudayda the week before, and five people in the other car had been killed. As the accident was his fault he had to come up with the "blood money" to pay the family of the people killed. The cousin's family was obligated to help him come up with the money. While we were there the men of the family met to decide how much each family member would pay. I have no idea what kind of money we're talking about. If the cousin failed to come up with the money, the wronged family could kill him to avenge their family deaths. This custom is the biggest reason why Peace Corps won't allow us to drive in Yemen.

We didn't arrive back in Hajja until 9:30 that night. Ibrahim's wife was waiting for us with a light supper. She had wanted to go to Mayben with us, but Ibrahim didn't want her to go as she wouldn't have been able to eat and chew qat with the men, and our trip would have been restricted more. Holly and I felt sorry that she had been left out. We didn't realize this until we returned; otherwise we would have asked for her to come with us. She wanted to do something special with us, and we allowed her to paint our hands with henna. I swore I would never have that done again because it takes months to disappear, but we didn't have the heart to turn her down. She thought she was doing something wonderful for us. So she put the henna (like mud) on our hands, wrapped them in plastic bags and put us to bed for the night wrapped up. We couldn't even take off our clothes.

The next morning, she removed the henna and put some black stuff on to turn the orange henna black. We had to sit with this stuff on for a couple of hours and hold our hands over live coals to burn the stuff in. It was very hot, and Holly and I kept pulling our hands away. She thought we were cowardly because she could touch the coals with her hands. Finally we were done! Now I have ten black fingertips to the first knuckle and black fingernails. I look like a member of a satanic cult. At noontime on Saturday, we left Hajja by taxi to return to Sana'a. It was a great trip.

Things continue to be quiet in Sana'a. We've heard that the socialist vice president will be returning to Sana'a from Aden as a truce has been worked out between the two sides. We'll see. Twenty-three new volunteers were sworn in at the Ambassador's residence last week. It was a nice affair, and we had a big party afterwards at the Peace Corps Director's house.

The last couple of days, I have been helping two of the older volunteers move into their apartment near the University. I've gone with them on shopping trips to get furniture and things. Some of my students from the University stopped to visit me so I drafted them to help us shop and carry things into their apartment. We had a great time.

PCV's are now going outside of Sana'a to teach in other cities. Holly is going to Aden; Eric is going to Ibb, one of the most colorful places in Yemen. I have the feeling of being on borrowed time, but then life itself is borrowed time.

Until next time,

October 8, 1992

Greetings Everyone,

This letter is being carried to the States by our new ET (early termination) person, Holly, the woman I traveled to Hajja with. She hated Aden and the situation at the university there. Since Peace Corps could not offer her another post, she decided to return to California.

The 26th of September was the celebration of the beginning of the Yemeni Revolution. It is similar to our 4th of July. Fireworks were set off all over the city. I had a great view of the fireworks from Muriel and June's high rise apartment near the Old University. Muriel and June are two new older volunteers from Colorado and California. It's wonderful to talk and spend time with people over 30! Of course, during the same celebration weekend, other bombs were bursting in air; one at the US Embassy where there was superficial damage, one aimed at the President's brother's house, and one at a leading politician's house. There was no serious damage done in any case. Otherwise, all is quiet.

Mainly these last few days I've wandered around Sana'a, especially the Old City, continuing to enjoy the romance of the place. As Muriel and June are still getting to know Sana'a, it's been fun showing them some of my favorite places and exploring new ones together. One day we took a dhabar to Hadda, a small village outside Sana'a, and walked through an orchard and up the steep steps to the top of the village from where we had a picturesque view of Sana'a in the distance and terraced fields below us. It was a very peaceful day without the blaring of car horns and the ever blowing dust of Sana'a. They have also been teaching me how to play bridge. I've always wanted to learn how, and now seems to be an appropriate time to learn.

An organization for American women living in Sana'a who wish to be involved with charity work is in the process of being formed. I went to the initial meeting a couple of weeks ago to find out what they're all about. The American Ambassador's wife, Mrs. Hughes, is one of the prime movers of the organization. Hopefully, it won't be just a coffee drinking organization. Dues will be $40 a year which is very expensive for Peace Corps people; so I want to see what they're really going to be about before I fork over the money. I'm going to go to an informational meeting this coming Sunday to talk about the Women's Center and learn their intentions.

We were supposed to begin registering students this coming Saturday, but the process has been delayed a week because a big book fair is in the progress, and our rooms are being used for the fair. If Allah is willing, we will begin to register students on the 17th of October. Such is the life of a Peace Corps teacher. But I'm not complaining.

Muriel (center) and June (right) in their apartment with PCV Rose

The nights are getting a little cooler now, the only sign that a new season is beginning. The days continue to be hot and dry, very pleasant weather. It doesn't seem possible that in another month I'll have been living in Yemen for a year. Life here seems very normal to me now, the exotic life in the streets: dust, garbage, sheep, goats, veiled women, men in zennas wearing jambhias and toting AK-47's over their shoulders and bombs bursting in air. What was life like before Peace Corps? For the first time since I've been here I've become conscious of how strange re-entry to the States will be. I think the hardest thing will be to listen to cutting remarks about Arabs. I have made many friends in Yemen, and although their customs are not mine, I have come to respect the Yemeni people and their approach to life.

One conversation I had with Muhammad Mokbel the beginning of the summer has become fixed in my thoughts. He asked me what my very first idea about Arabs was. I had to travel far back in time to my childhood. I couldn't remember having a specific thought about Arabs; I just remembered that my first idea had something to do with Arabs being a violent, untrustworthy people. My impression was negative. I turned Muhammad's question around and asked him his first impression of Americans. He said he thought Americans were his enemies. We both decided that we have traveled a long way since our first impressions of each other's culture. How little I studied about this part of the world in school, how slanted the journalists are in their reporting about the Arab World. There is much about life here that is strange to me, much about the lives of women particularly that I find sad. But there is so much about the gentle, caring friendship of Yemeni people that I love. Therein lays the main reason, as far as I'm concerned, for Peace Corps. I will learn much more than I'll ever teach. If this country dissolves into civil war, real people will be killed and hurt, people I've come to care about.

With money my friend Joanne sent me I went to the suq and bought serwals (the pants women wear under dresses) for little girls who come to the Women's Center. As most of our donated clothes come from Westerners, we have no serwals to give little girls who have to cover their legs. The day I took them to the Center there were many girls who came in, and it was fun giving Joanne's pants to them. I got twenty pairs of pants with your money, Joanne. I carry money converted into riyals from Arlene's sister Kathleen with me as I travel around Sana'a. When I see very sad beggars with children who look as if they came from Somalia or the Sudan (which is also enmeshed in war with a growing number of starving refugees) I give them 50 to 100 riyals, enough to live on for one or two days. Yesterday, I gave money to a sad family of five, four children under seven or eight and a young mother sleeping on the street. The other day I gave 100 riyals to a mother nursing her child in Bab al-Yemen. I'm going to give 100 riyals to Yahya who is trying to save money so that he can marry his cousin who came from Somalia a few months ago. I think Katherine would want me to use the money to help refugees celebrate life as well as save lives.

A refugee family

Khalid came to see me yesterday to tell me his grandmother had died. On the third day after a family member dies (the person is buried the day of death) a sheep or cow is slaughtered and the neighbors of the deceased are invited to eat. If the neighbors are rich then it is appropriate to find poor people and give the meat to them. Khalid asked me how to get to Mahwar as he wants to give some of the meat to those refugees who come to the Women's Center. I was touched that Khalid had obviously taken to heart my stories of the people who live there and wanted to help. He is an impresive young man who wants so much to learn and help his country. I hope he can one day study in the States. If anyone has any suggestion of a group that would like to sponsor a deserving, intelligent 18 year old Yemeni man, you couldn't find a better candidate. He is so open to learning, very curious about the West, but he is also loyal to his country and would return to Yemen, I think, to help his country.

I am also impressed with Khalid because he recognizes that the lives of women must be improved. He doesn't want to marry an uneducated woman from the village. He wants a wife who will be his equal, his partner. I don't think he is just telling me that to please me. He has shared some personal thoughts and concerns that convince me of his sincerity. Unfortunately, although there are scholarship programs here to study abroad, the rumor is that you have to be well connected to have the Yemeni government nominate you. There is much corruption and bribe money in the country.

An example of the corruption in Yemen can be illustrated by the story that Khalid told me recently. A meter reader told Khalid that the meter on his family's house was defective and was not properly recording their electricial consumption. He told Khalid that he would fix it and say nothing to the company if Khalid would give him 400 riyals. Khalid refused to give the man the money because his family had done nothering wrong. Khalid said that the meter should be replaced, and if his family owed money for back electricity, they would pay what they owed. So the meter reader left angry and returned a little later with a man form the electric company who cut off the electricity to Khalid's house. As it was the long September 26th weekend, they were without electricity for three days. On Sunday, Khalid went to the company and complained to the manager. The manager said that if Khalid gave him 1000 riyals, he would take care of the matter. Again Khalid refused to pay the bribe money. To make the story short, Khalid's family eventually had to pay 6000 riyals to get their electricity turned back on. They were accused of tampering with the meter and the 6000 was the fine; they would still have to pay to have the meter fixed. A high price for honesty. At least Khalid's father told him that he did the right thing.
So that's all for now folks. I don't have much to report in this letter which is a little dull. Perhaps my life is becoming too routine.

Happy Halloween,

October 27, 1992

Dear Friends & Family,

By the time this letter reaches you I'm sure it will be almost Thanksgiving as the person who is delivering the letter to the States is first traveling to Thailand with her husband. So even though my news will be a little late by the time it reaches you, I'm taking advantage of all the opportunities to send letters home.
I bet you picture me already in school teaching, right? Guess again. This whole month has been a farce as far as teaching is concerned. I've been assigned to the new campus to teach with three other volunteers. Two of them are new volunteers, one a recent graduate from Simonds College in Boston, the other a 60ish retired principal from California. It's the same distance from my home to my new classroom.

The first time we reported to work we couldn't get in the building, which is a large relatively new classroom building that houses mainly the law faculty. Because there was a big book fair in progress that was set up in our classrooms, we waited for the fair to end ten days later, and reported again. The first floor where our classes were supposed to be held was a disaster area. The rooms were filled with rubbish and were VERY DIRTY. There were no chairs in the rooms. Although the book fair had been over for several days, the custodial staff hadn't gotten around to cleaning the rooms. To further complicate matters, the rooms had all been renumbered, and we didn't know where we were supposed to teach as our room assignments no longer existed. So we said we would come back to work when we had rooms.
Over the last weekend (October 22nd and 23rd) unused classrooms were found for us. What a mess they were. Chairs were piled in the back of the room. There was at least a quarter inch of dirt on the floor and paper scraps, cigarette butts, old soda bottles, and sticky stains left by over turned soda and tea. But the rooms were ours. We reported to work on Saturday with mops, broom, buckets, and rags. We spent four hours cleaning up three very filthy rooms that hadn't been used for some time.

Several students stopped by for class and instead watched us work. They were surprised to see American teachers cleaning the rooms. Some of them helped us take out the broken chairs and clean the rooms. They told us we shouldn't be doing the cleaning ourselves, but we've learned that if it's going to get done, we have to do it. I gave a woman who was passing a broom through the hallway some riyals to sweep my room. This may have been a good first teaching lesson about the failure of all cast systems. Even though we are teachers, we shouldn't be afraid to get our hands dirty. Yemeni teachers would not clean their rooms. One of the students walked me out of the building when I had finished and told me he thought Americans were good people. That was nice to hear.

So the rooms are fairly clean by Yemeni standards. American teachers would think of the rooms as being dirty. But we did the best we could with cold water to eliminate years of crud. Actually, the rooms are quite pleasant, big and light. We have keys for our rooms so we intend to keep them locked when we are not there. We're afraid that some of the professors will discover the newly cleaned rooms and want to use them, too. If we have to share them, they will soon be trashed again. Americans sure do have a different attitude toward cleanliness.

I like my room a lot. It has a green chalk board in both the back and the front of the room and four large windows that look out onto a fairly nice campus scene, not as nice as last year's view at the Old University, however. I'll teach two hour and a half classes daily, one at 10 and the other at 12, four days a week. Each of my four classes will meet twice a week. The lesson plan is the same for all of them which means I have to prepare only two lesson plans a week. Since I don't have classes on Wednesdays, I'll work at the Women's Center. Thursday and Friday are weekend days and therefore free. All looks fine at the moment, but one never knows here.

In my classroom

Three women students

I'm standing with some of my women students

Have classes started? You ask. No way. We are now registering students, and if all goes well, classes will begin October 31st. The semester will end sometime in January. Our semester will probably be about ten weeks long, more like a marking period than a semester. But who knows what will transpire. Will there be a break during the November elections? Will the elections be postponed because of the unrest in the country? No one knows. We are all trying to remember the most important Peace Corps word, FLEXIBILITY.

It's nice to see the students back on campus, especially my four horsemen who have been gone most of the summer. Yassin and Abdul Basset came by for tea this afternoon. Yassin told me that he wants to stick to me all year, be my brother, an adopted son, so that he can really improve his English. In exchange he will provide any service he can for me. I really enjoy their company a great deal. I told them that soon I want to go back to the little restaurant where we ate the blackened fish last spring.

One rainy night a couple of weeks ago, Yahya picked me up in his brother-in-law's truck and drove me to his sister's house to meet his family. Of course I only met the women: his mother, sister, an infant, his nieces and the cousin he hopes to marry this winter if he can find a job and save enough money to buy a bedroom. The job he had didn't work out. Don't ask me to explain. I suppose a bedroom will be added to the house and Yahya will have to furnish it.

The sister's house was very simple, but not as poorly furnished as I feared. We didn't visit the mother's house, which was close by, as the rain made it impossible to visit. I suspect that it must have been raining in the house. The women went out of their way to serve me. I ate falafel and four kinds of honey sweetened desserts that were a little too sweet for my taste. But, as they were disappointed with my lack of appetite I ate one of each of the desserts they had especially made for me. Because they continued to be disappointed in my lack of appetite, I ate one of each again. Yahya was the only person to eat with me because the mother and sister were fasting because they hadn't fasted during Ramadan. The sister was pregnant at that time and couldn't fast; the cousin was in the process of escaping from Somalia through Ethiopia and eventually to the boats that took them to Aden. I don't know why the mother was fasting because she was in Aden during Ramadan. As I worked my way through the food they had prepared for me, one at a time they prayed on the floor beside me. A strange experience. I was the first American to visit them, and I think the visit went well. They are very warm, kind people. They have endured much uprooting and tragedy. My life seems so simple and uncomplicated by comparison. Anyway, I feel honored that Yahya took me to meet his family, and he said that I did well with my Arabic.

At the time I was at Yahya's sister's house, the cousin hadn't been told of her future plans to marry Yahya. But Yahya told me a few days ago that his uncle had told her she will marry Yahya. I asked him if she was happy about it. He gave me a strange look and said, "Of course!" Poor girl. She will probably be a mother by the time she is 15. Yahya who is 22 is very anxious to have children he told me. I gave him 150 riyals from Arlene's sister Kathleen and told him the money was from a friend in America who wants to help the Somalia refugees.

I find Khalid, my Arabic tutor, an exceptionally honest and dedicated young man of 18. He also has a great sense of humor which makes him fun to spend time with. Khalid wants to study in the West, preferably America, so he can learn about democracy, business, and computers. He has the soul of a poet. He likes to borrow my classical tapes and listen to Western music. He is frustrated with Yemeni schools and the learning by rote method he is forced to endure.

I told him that life in the States would be very different and that he would see people his age drinking and living a very different life than his in Yemen. Unmarried men and women socialize together. Khalid has never kissed a girl. I also told him that there might be people who will dislike him because he is an Arab and that unless he is in a big city there won't be many Muslims around. He told me "I know that. I think religion belongs to God and the earth to the People."

The weather continues to be beautiful. The nights are decidedly cooler, but the days are warm. I am reminded of Indian summer at home. I wonder if I will find the winter colder this year than I did last year as I have had a whole year now to adjust to Sana'a weather. I can't say enough positive things about the endless beautiful days.

All appears to be quiet on the political scene. I ran into Ahmed, a former student from practice teaching whom I have chewed qat with periodically. Ahmed is a captain fighter pilot in the Air Force. He told me that he is almost always on duty because of the "problems". But he doesn't think that the country is going to blow up any more. There will probably be problems and little battles, but Yemenis know that they have too much to lose if war erupts, he thinks. I think I am getting used to this whatever-Allah-wills life.

As I said in the beginning of the letter, this probably won't reach you much before Thanksgiving. You will all be in my thoughts that day as you are every day. I have a lot to be thankful for this year; good family and friends, good health, and an incredible adventure. I'll be coming home in just 15 months. Enjoy doing the Thanksgiving dishes!!

All for now folks,

Khalid Muhammad Al-Yabari

November 23, 1992

Happy Thanksgiving Everyone,

By the time this letter reaches you the dishes will be done and the good turkey all digested. We're going to have dinner at the Peace Corps Director's house. At this point we're hoping it will be turkey that we're served. However, there appears to be a shortage of turkeys in Yemen. Some turkeys were shipped for Americans, but Peace Corps Volunteers are the step-children of the American community and, therefore, the last in line for turkeys. Cecilia Hitte, our director, is working on the problem.

Sorry I've been so long about writing. But I have been busy for a change. That is, classes finally began at the University the beginning of November. All my classes have 60 students in them, and most of the students show up for class this year. Although my room is big, the students are jammed in. You can imagine how effective a teacher must be teaching a language class to 60 students. Obviously the only way to have them practice speaking much is choral speaking. I try to call on as many students as possible. The women sit on the right side of the room, mostly veiled to the eyeballs. The men sit on the left of the center aisle wearing either western or Yemeni clothes.

I really am enjoying the students very much. They are excited about studying English with an American. At least that's what they tell me. They follow me around when I am in the classroom building buying me tea and offering to be of any service to me. I love the fact that they never say they are bored and are willing to participate in any activity I ask them to do. We laugh a lot, too. The first day of classes I had the students introduce themselves. One student, Hussein, said at the end of his introduction, "I am from Iraq, and I hope you won't think of me as your enemy." We had a little heart to heart talk after class and decided to leave the wars to our governments.

I really do enjoy teaching here. I haven't felt this way about teaching for a long time. I am glad I can end my teaching career feeling so positive about it. Here in the Developing World the importance of education is still realized and respected. However, Yemeni teachers are angry because the foreign teachers are paid more money. There is a perception that if you are foreign you must be a better teacher. Mass education only began in earnest here in the late 1960's which might account for the distrust of Yemeni teachers in general. But attitudes are changing, I'm told. I willingly buy my own chalk and attempt to teach 60 students in a class because it is fun. I wouldn't trade classrooms with anyone I know at home. By the way though, if anyone has any posters they are willing to part with, I would love to have them for my classroom to put on my bare walls. Skiing posters would be great or any winter scenes especially as they don't know about snow. But any posters would be wonderful as I need some color in my classroom.

As most of you can imagine, I was overjoyed with the election of Bill Clinton after twelve sad years of Republicans. I was 38 the last time we had a Democrat in the White House. I was trying to follow the election predictions on VOA the last couple of weeks before the election. The commentators kept saying it was too close to call. So the landslide came as a surprise here. The day after the election (it was still election eve at home) we got up at 4am and went to the Taj Sheba hotel, and for a couple of hours we were back in the USA. A room had been set up with American flags; four TV's were tuned to CNN and other major networks; a huge American map was used to track the election results as reported on TV. It was truly amazing. Seeing familiar commentators and watching scenes from home was exciting. The American Embassy put on the event for Americans living here. We also had coffee and pastries.

Of course the embassy officials and the American Ambassador and his wife were very disappointed with the results because they are mostly political appointees who will have to resign. I confess that although I tried to be polite, I didn't try to mask my delight with the results. As you might guess, the Yemeni people are delighted that President Bush lost as he is very unpopular here because of the Gulf War. I hope President Clinton is more sensitive to the concerns and opinions of Arabs, especially concerning the Palestine problem.

One morning a couple of weeks ago I woke up to the excited chatter of my roommates. Fran had found a rat doing the breast stroke in the toilet bowl. She slammed the cover and weighted it down with a heavy bag of beans. As neither Beth nor Fran could deal with dueling the rat, I decided I had to try. So I dressed in my combat wear (black sweat suit) and armed myself with a sieve to scoop the intruder out of the toilet and into the toilet paper bucket. It took me several minutes to get up my courage to lift the cover. When I did, I found the bowl empty. Evidently he had turned around and crawled back down the pipes to the great Sana'a sewer, which must be quite a place. We kept flushing the toilet and pouring disinfectant down to discourage his return. We haven't seen him since, but let me tell you, I no longer sit down on the seat in the middle of the night with the lights off!

Last Thursday, November 19th, Muriel, June, Rose (three new volunteers) and I went to Ma'rib to see the dam and other points of historical interest, including Baraquish. As you may remember, I visited Ma'rib last April soon after my return from the States. As it is an impressive trip I was happy to go there with the others who wanted to explore the area.

Yahya finally found a taxi to drive from someone and is very happy to have a job. He can help his family and get married soon. He has to pay the owner of the taxi 300 riyals a day and pay for all the gas and oil as well as routine maintenance. The money after his cost of maintaining the taxi is his. So I asked him if he would be interested in driving us to Ma'rib. He was delighted to have the opportunity.

Foolishly, I never questioned his driving ability. I had driven around Sana'a with him and thought he would be up to the task of driving us. He ran the first military check point and we were fined 100 riyals. When he started to descend down the mountain to the desert, I realized he knew nothing about driving in the mountains. He didn't shift down; he rode his brake the whole way. The brakes began to smell, so I decided to give him a polite driving lesson because I was afraid the brakes would lock or burn out. Fortunately, we made it. But I could tell he was shook up as he continued to drive VERY slowly even after we reached the flat straight driving of the desert.

We stopped in Baraquish , the ancient city ruins dating back to the 9th Century AD perched on a little knoll in the desert. It was very impressive the second time. Bedouins guard the ruins and try to get tips from tourists.

Tower Ruins in Baraquish　　　*Yahya at Baraquish*

Yahya wasn't careful about staying on the dirt road and drove off into loose sand. We were stuck. He madly spun the wheels, and I couldn't make him understand about rocking the car so I told him to get out and I would drive. We were deep in the sand. We tried putting rocks and the floor mats under the tires, but we couldn't get the car out. Finally about ten Bedouins carrying their AK-47's came to our rescue. Strong Bedouin power was what finally freed the car with me driving. I wondered for a moment if they would steal the car as that is a favorite sport in that area. However, I think the car and all of us looked too miskeene (Arabic word meaning poor, pathetic, beggar) to bother to steal it.

Rose, Muriel, and June with our Bedouin rescuers helping get the car out

By this time I was concerned about Yahya's driving ability because when we started off for Ma'rib his weaving all over the road made me very nervous. He admitted to feeling dizzy and sick because of the drive down the mountain. I decided that even though it is against Peace Corps rules and grounds for immediate dismissal I would drive for a while. I knew that we would be in trouble with the soldiers at the frequent check points, but it was better for me to drive than to let Yahya continue. Fortunately, we switched drivers before the next check point and escaped certain trouble. But bigger trouble lay ahead.

After having lunch, we drove to the Old Ma'rib Dam. It is truly impressive to look at the two remaining sections, over 2000 years old that still stand. Rose, an old rock climber, couldn't resist the challenge and tried to scale one wall. She nearly made it to the top (around 20 feet tall) when she planted her foot on a loose rock and went tumbling down. Her right leg was obviously broken and the left leg was questionable. I was worried about her back as well. But she felt it was okay so I lifted her head enough to place my sweater under it. We sent Yahya and June in the car to try to get some people in a land rover to come help us. They refused to help because Yemenis won't help people in an accident as they are afraid of being sued if the injured person dies.

Meanwhile, Muriel stayed with Rose, keeping the sun out of her eyes and comforting her as I searched the desert for sticks that we could use as splints for her legs. There are not sticks in the desert! I could only find dead cacti branches with long sharp needles. Finally we found some branches with the needles gone. Fortunately they were still green enough not to break easily when they were tied around her legs with Yahya's belt and Muriel's sweater. Rose is a health worker in Hajja and knew more about medicine than the rest of us. She directed us, telling us what to do. She was in deep pain, but she kept her cool and an amazing show of strength and courage. I was worried about putting her in the taxi as I didn't know how we would be able to stretch her out as the back seat wasn't long enough. Also, how could we ever get her in without doing more damage to her legs? I wasn't sure her back was okay. The trip back to Sana'a was between 3 and 4 hours. Even if there was a hospital in Ma'rib I decided we could not take her to it as the medical practices here are medieval at best.

As we were about to start dragging her to the car, two land rovers drove up. One was filled with a French group. I tried to ask them for help, but the shock of all that had transpired made what French I knew disappear. I couldn't remember a word in French. Only Arabic words came. They didn't speak English. The Yemeni driver said there was absolutely no way they could help. The other land rover had a Swiss couple in it. They spoke good English and told us that we could take their land rover back to Sana'a if Yahya would stay overnight with them at their hotel in Ma'rib and drive them back to Sana'a the next day. Their driver didn't want to do that, but they insisted. Thank God!! Everyone helped us slip a blanket taken from the land rover under Rose and carry her to the rover and lift her in. This was no easy task as Rose is a big woman. I knew her ankle was in bad shape so I carried her foot during this process. I almost got sick when I picked it up as I could tell it wasn't attached by much. June and Yahya couldn't make decisions; they didn't know what to do. Muriel was great, helpful, supportive and filled in when I needed a break. June, Muriel and I got into the land rover with Rose who was stretched out on the floor in the back and left Yahya behind with the wonderfully generous Swiss couple who had no idea what a bad driver Yahya was.

I told the driver that I wanted to call the American Embassy before we started back to Sana'a to report the accident and to alert them so the American doctor would be ready to help when we arrived and secondly to receive some medical advice about how to take care of Rose on the long trip. Rose wanted a pain killer which I was afraid to buy at a local pharmacy because I didn't know anything about such medicine and the directions would be in Arabic. Also, I was afraid she would go into shock. She had lain in the sun on the desert for an hour and a half. The Marine guard I talked to at the Embassy told me that the American doctor was out of the county and that it would take at least 10 to 15 minutes to get the information I wanted from BJ, the nurse who was on call. I told him we didn't have time to spare. We were going to the Embassy and would be there in 3 to 4 hours.

"What do I do to keep her from going into shock?" I asked.

"Just keep her comfortable, warm and talking," he said.

So I sat scrunched up in the back of the land rover with Rose, talking to her the whole time. We relived the 60's, talked about what she thinks of Clinton. She was from Arkansas and although Philosophically a Republican, said that Clinton was a good man she knows personally as does everyone else in Arkansas. We made great time and arrived in Sana'a in two and a half hours. I didn't tell anyone in the car that the doctor was out of the country as I thought that would add panic to the situation.

When we arrived at the Embassy, I talked to Rob, the Marine guard on the phone. He told me we had to go to a Yemeni hospital so that Rose could have x-rays taken. My heart sank as I thought that if we could just get her to the clinic in the Embassy all would be taken care of. He said we could go there and meet BJ, the nurse, if we wished. I said no; I thought it important that Rose be accompanied to the hospital with an American medical officer. So he ordered the guards to check the land rover for bombs and weapons (the driver had to turn over his jambiya). Then we were allowed to drive into the Embassy compound.

While we waited for BJ to arrive, our driver demanded to be paid $200 for his services. I couldn't believe it. I knew he had been paid by the Swiss couple, and we expected to tip him 300 riyals. When I offered him the money, he refused to take it. He wanted the $200 he said. Remember, I only earn a little over $200 a month. But he thought we were rich Americans that he could charge an unreasonable price for humanitarian services. The Swiss couple had already paid $450 for the car and 3000 riyals for the driver, we later learned from Yahya. He refused to drive Rose to the hospital so when BJ arrived Rose had to be moved from the land rover to the Embassy land rover. Obviously, this was painful for Rose. I was furious with the driver and had to back out of the situation or hit him. Then we started for Al-Thora hospital, the best hospital in Sana'a.

When we arrived at the emergency door we had to wait as other patients were unloaded from cars. There was no hospital gurney available. They were carrying people into the hospital on bed springs. Rose was carried in on the Marine stretcher. The corridors were very crowded. I lead the way, making a path for the stretcher being carried by BJ's husband and three Yemenis who worked at the Embassy. The Marines could not leave the Embassy unguarded. Rose was carried into the x-ray room and placed on the table. The room was filled with other patients and their families. People were moaning and crying. Muriel, June and I waited outside in the corridor. I was so happy when Abdullah, the Peace Corps Administrative Officer, came up to us. He told us that Cecilia was on the way. Meanwhile, the driver from Ma'rib came into the corridor where we were standing and stood in the corridor with us. He was still demanding his $200.

Finally Rose was wheeled out of x-ray on a gurney that had been found. She was placed in the corridor with us. The doctor, Cecilia, Rose, the three of us as well as assorted Yemenis, including soldiers with their AK-47's, other patients and workers, looked at the x-rays of Rose's legs that the doctor held up to the lights. She would need an operation to pin her badly broken ankle the doctor said. Cecilia said she would have to call Washington to see what they said. The doctor said that it was impossible to make a long distance call from the hospital, so Cecilia, the doctor, and BJ went to the Peace Corps office to call Washington while BJ's husband Ken, Muriel and I stayed with Rose who had finally been given some morphine. June went home. BJ left me in charge of the pocketbook she was carrying that had morphine in it. She told me to guard the pocketbook with my life as the Yemenis would love to get ahold of it. They don't have pain killers like that in the hospital.

We waited for over two hours for them to return. Rose was cold and there weren't any blankets for patients in emergency. Ken finally got a soldier to let Rose borrow his blanket for a price. We stood guarding her on the gurney. People stared at her, came up to her and blew smoke in her face. She had no privacy. Corpses were wheeled by us. Bloodied people kept coming into emergency.

Finally the group came back from the Peace Corps office and said that the Washington doctors wanted her to return to Washington for the operation. I was relieved because the chaos and filth in the hospital made me nervous. While she went to have casts put on both feet, BJ went to the Embassy to get blankets and supplies because Rose was going to have to stay the night in the hospital. When BJ returned we took Rose to her private room on the fourth floor. Muriel and I had to stay with her to make sure no Yemeni doctor or nurse did anything to her or gave her any medicine. BJ wanted her only to receive the medicine she gave her. When we moved her into her bed a whole bunch of Yemenis came in to watch. We had to shoo them out so Rose could use the bed pan BJ had brought from the Embassy. Our other purpose for being there was to guard the things BJ had brought for Rose and us. Thank goodness she brought a lot of blankets because it was cold. I slept on the gurney and Muriel slept on the other bed. Actually we only slept from 3 to 5am. At 5am we were awakened by an incredible popping sound. It sounded like firecrackers or machine guns. The tiles on the floor all started to pop up. We don't know why. But what a sound. At 11am, June and my roommate Fran came with Cecilia to relieve Muriel and me. Later that day Rose was moved to the Embassy.

At 2am this morning she began her long flight back to Washington, DC and to George Washington Hospital. We all hope she will recover soon and be able to return to complete her tour. This whole experience still seems unreal, and I dream about it at night. The positive thing is that it made those of us who went through the desert madness close, especially Muriel and me. I have finally been tested under fire.

We had our one year anniversary party a couple of weeks ago. Meanwhile, two more volunteers have resigned. I am working Wednesdays at the Women's Center. We're very busy these days. The number of refugees seems to be growing. More refugees from Somalia keep arriving. The political situation is still shaky. The November elections were postponed until April. Many Yemeni people are upset about the postponement. A big strike was called for yesterday as a protest. The strike was cancelled, probably because of government pressure. Air Force planes fly over Sana'a every night.

I am active in the newly formed American Women's Group. I'm on the community service committee. We are going to be working on a project to help to pay for poor Yemeni children's primary education. We hope to sponsor more girls as girls are considered such throw away items here. On the third of December we are having a Christmas bazar at the Embassy to raise money for our project. We will sell the baskets and clothes made at the Center, among other things.

I think I've recovered from my six week bout with giardia that I think I got when I was in Hajja. The good thing about the prolonged diarrhea was the loss of another ten pounds. So that's all for this month folks.

Take care,

December 9, 1992

Greetings Everyone,

Merry Christmas! I trust this letter will reach you before the 25th. One of the volunteers is returning home for Christmas as she has a month break from YALI, the Yemen American Language Institute, where she teaches. Her parents bought her the plane ticket for her Christmas present. Since I'm teaching at the University, there will be no Christmas break because it is not a recognized holiday. Fortunately, Christmas is on a Friday, a weekend day in Yemen.

Sharon Firnam, a woman I met in the American Women's Group, is returning to the States with her husband for Christmas and has asked me if I would house sit for them. I JUMPED AT THE CHANCE! Can you imagine I'll actually get to stay in a house with an oven, microwave, TV, VCR, and I hope most of all a good stereo system. I still have to go over the details with her, but as it stands now, I'll be moving in the 16th or 17th of December and staying until the end of January. What a nice vacation. I can't wait to have some space to myself and indulge in the luxuries. Sharon told me one of the reasons they would like to have me stay in their apartment is to keep the maid on her toes. I probably will return home one day a week because it is closer to the University, and I have Arabic lessons Tuesday evenings.

We had a great Thanksgiving. Fran, Eric (the young volunteer stationed in IBB I've written about who stays at our house when he comes to Sana'a) and I went to Muriel and June's apartment for brunch. I fried some peppers, bisbas (chilies), onions, and tomatoes and cooked them in an omelet. Muriel fried up a can of bacon that one of the embassy wives had given us that we were saving for a special event. We had a feast. I can't tell you how good the bacon tasted. I wanted to shout over the roof tops of Sana'a that I was eating unclean meat and loving every bit of it. Muriel saved the bacon fat that she will use to fry chicken in some day. She will make the famous Southern fried chicken because she was originally from South Carolina. After brunch we played bridge.

Late in the afternoon we went to Cecilia's house where we were all invited for Thanksgiving Dinner. It was a delicious feast. There was a nice bar setup for us, and I enjoyed a couple of glasses of red wine. I hadn't had any red wine since I was home in March. What a treat. For an after dinner drink I had a B&B. Wonderful!

The meal centered around two turkeys that were beautifully cooked. I enjoyed the turkey, mashed potatoes and gravy, cranberry sauce, and brussel sprouts the most. There were many appetizing desserts that I never tasted as I chose to have seconds on turkey and the fixings instead. Before we ate, the thirty plus of us stood around the buffet table and toasted each other and those of you at home in as many languages and traditional greetings as we could remember. It was indeed an enjoyable, memorable Thanksgiving.

I have eaten lunch out a couple of times with the Four Horsemen, once at a local salta joint. They brought tomatoes, chilies, onions, and a can of mackerel with them and asked the cook to add the ingredients to the salta. It was the best salta I've eaten. Maybe I'm finally getting used to the unfamiliar taste of helba. They have also taken me to a couple of bazaars on Friday afternoons. The bazaars are a little like fairs, but with not much to see or do except talk and watch people.

I treated the horsemen and Khalid, my tutor, to the play, YOU'RE A GOOD MAN CHARLIE BROWN, put on by a local amateur group of ex-pats. It was a good production, and they again were enchanted with seeing Western theater. Khalid had never seen a Western play. It was very rewarding for me to watch his excitement.

The giardia I wrote about in my last letter has returned with a vengeance and the diarrhea and vomiting kept me from going to the University for a week. The doctor has put me on a triple dose of flagyl to knock it out of my system. It's been unpleasant, but I'll live. I've had diarrhea more this past year than in my whole life put together. Part of the experience of living in the Developing World! Much of the PCVs' conversation with each other centers around our digestive systems. One hardly mentions diarrhea at home, but here it as normal as talking about what you ate for dinner because we all deal with the problem. Unfortunately, the giardia kept me from attending the annual Christmas reception at the American Embassy. I had been looking forward to it as I enjoyed it so much last year. But I did get to see the Embassy Christmas decorations at the American Women's Group bazaar held there on the 3rd of December. The Women's Center sold 15,000 riyals worth of things, mainly baskets and cloth things the women had sewn. The Yemeni women are so excited. The bazaar also made the American community aware of the Women's Center and what goes on there. It makes me feel good to be a part of the American Women's Group and the Women's Center. Last night I went to the annual Christmas concert performed by mainly British and American singers. It was warm and nice to be celebrating Christmas. Certainly for me the journey of the Three Wise men bringing frankincense and myrrh has a new meaning for me as this is where the incense came from.

Rumor has it that our semester will end the first week of January. We still haven't heard whether or not we are supposed to give midterms. This coming week we're going to give one anyway. Then if it isn't going to count, it's good practice for the students. If the rumor is true, we will give our final exam sometime in January and spend at least two weeks correcting exams and tabulating grades. We don't know what our semester break will be or when. One rumor is that we will have a two week break the end of January, beginning of February. The second semester will begin for a week then take Ramadan off which begins February 23rd or 24th. Another rumor is that the University will be closed February and March. The third rumor is that the University will be closed for February and open in March during Ramadan even though students won't attend classes. One of these days we'll find out what the plan is. It is just difficult to make travel plans because it is all so indefinite.

Now, would you expect the University or government to have an AIDS awareness campaign? I'm sure there must be people with AIDS here given the growing number of refugees entering the country from Africa. But the health problems of aids, cholera and typhoid are not publicly addressed as far as I can tell. The University is not on any computer system; everything is still done by hand or with typewriters that are ancient. I have no access to a supply closet or a place to run off tests. Fran's project has been to try to get the language lab functioning. It already exists, but it is dirty and unused. Why? Again a lesson to be learned about sending money to have things done in the Developing World unless you send the people who are going to run the program and train people to use the equipment it is wasted money. Most of the teaching is done here in turn of the century style: chalk, blackboard, memorize, recite. Textbooks are hard to come by. I saw the books of a first year medical student that are in English. They are Xeroxed copies. Now everyone knows science is not my favorite or best subject, but I could easily read and comprehend the scientific principles discussed in his books. Does that tell you anything?

A couple of weeks ago the black market money changers in the suq were closed down by the government and put in jail. The dollar was soaring into the area of 40 riyals to the dollar, and the rumor was that it would soon reach 60 riyals to the dollar. The official government rate recognized by the banks is 18 riyals to the dollar. Closing the black market and putting the dealers in jail is a way to control inflation. Can we learn something from this method? Anyway, you can still change money on the black market. I've heard that if you wander in the suq, people will approach you, or you can get a Yemeni you trust to change money as they will go to a home of one of the jailed money changers.

I am going to change dollars into riyals soon as I am finding it almost impossible to live on the Peace Corps monthly allotment. The dollar buys a lot of riyals. But I'm paid in riyals based on the official government rate of exchange. Prices are going up. Yes, I could cut down on some things. I didn't have to treat the Horsemen and Khalid to the play. But they have treated me to many things, and I can't keep accepting without doing something for them. We hope that Peace Corps will make an adjustment, but at this point it seems doubtful and will probably take a year to work through the red tape.

I chewed qat and smoked the mada'a recently with Cecilia and a couple of her friends at her house. An enjoyable afternoon. I hadn't chewed for a couple of months. It's too bad Cecilia is my boss and a very busy person as I would enjoy her friendship otherwise. She's an interesting, strong woman.

As Christmas approaches I am reflecting on all that has happened to me during this very eventful year. Certainly my life has been enriched and changed by all I have experienced. It has been exciting, difficult, challenging, lonely, and rewarding. I am so glad I've had the opportunity to live in Yemen for a year. Unless something happens, I should get to spend another year here. I can't, however, imagine the second year being more eye opening and broadening than this first year. As it is the season for reflection, I am thinking of home, my family and friends. I am homesick, but even that can be a positive experience. There are many things I won't take for granted again: a glass of good wine, bacon, ham, steak, a stove, broccoli, a meal in the North End of Boston, good music, movies, plays, the Red Sox, TV, clean streets with no dust and litter, good water, efficient toilets, a real bed, chairs, lobster, Doritos, flowers, trees, and most of all you, my friends and family. Then I think of the women and children I see at the Women's Center and realize how comfortable and rich I am. Sorry you won't receive any presents from me this year, but I am going to buy a bunch of flip flops for the barefoot children who come to the Center and give them in your names. I miss you all and wish you a Merry Christmas and Happy New Year.

Until next year,

January 20, 1993

Dear Friends and Family,

So, how's the rough winter treating you all? We hear that it is particularly cold in the good old USA this season. Here the sun continues to shine during the day and the nights are cool, probably somewhere in the 50's on really cold nights. Lately, the sun feels more intense during the day, a sign that spring is coming. Of course, there is heat of another kind here now with the continuing tribal battles that keep flaring up in shoot-outs, the Yemeni reaction to the bombing in Iraq, anger about the postponement yet again of the election to May, frustration with the soaring inflation, and the growing appeal of the Islamic Brotherhood party that is distrustful of Western influence. We understand that CNN is paying a lot of attention to this corner of the World, probably because of our troops in Somalia.

But, really, life is pretty normal for us. Remember, we move about the country in dhabars, local taxis and buses. So actually we are safer than the high profile ex-pats who drive around in well-marked land rovers. The violence that is going on here is not directed at us personally. Although today some individuals were passing out leaflets encouraging Yemenis to kill any Westerners they see in retribution for the bombings in Iraq. Yes, sometimes comments are made to us; some volunteers have been spit upon. But nothing serious has happened.

The other night I watched the Yemeni news in English and was heart sick at the pictures shown of the civilians killed and wounded in Bagdad by our bombs. You can imagine that the Yemeni version of CNN was pretty graphic. I don't know what I personally feel about it all, but it is a funny feeling to walk around a city where the people basically disapprove of your country's actions. It is so much easier to go through such an experience at home. For me Arabs are not a mass of nameless people. They have faces, families and friends; they have personalities. They are people, not a plague to be eliminated. Saddam may well deserve to be destroyed, but not all the innocent people caught up in this violence. I don't know the answer, but it is certainly more complicated than a John Wayne solution. When second semester begins, I wonder how my students, particularly my Iraqi and Palestinian students, will react to me.

We had a Peace Corps security meeting yesterday and have been assured that we are not in danger. We were told not to travel to some places in Yemen (Ma'rib is one hot spot to avoid, but I have no desire to go back there!) We were also told to stay away from some areas in Sana'a where demonstrations are likely to occur and, of course, to avoid large crowds. The present policy is to maintain a low profile which I am gladly doing as I have no aspirations to find myself in the middle of a shoot-out. We also learned at the meeting that Peace Corps is going to increase our salaries by 40% as it is difficult to live on our 6400 riyals a month. That is a great relief as the last two months I have had to cash dollars into riyals to make it. We will be receiving 8950 riyals a month in the near future. Remember, if any of you have any questions or concerns, call the Yemen desk, Peace Corps Washington. Someone at the Yemen desk talks to our director every day so that Washington can learn what is happening here. Just remember how the news media like to blow stories out of proportion.

Yesterday my vacation house sitting ended. It was a restful and pleasant reminder of what luxuries I used to enjoy. Most of all, I enjoyed listening to good music and washing my clothes in a real washing machine. I almost cried when I did my first load of laundry. The clothes came out so clean and so soft. The smell of Bounce was the nicest smell I've experienced in a long time.

Muriel, June, and Fran came to visit me for Christmas and New Year's. Eric and Artis also joined us. We dubbed it the "Golden Girls" Christmas. We bought some qat and put the branches in a pail of water. We decorated the "tree" with paper snowflakes, cotton batten, and tinsel that the embassy nurse gave to Muriel for tree decorating purposes. Our star was a little Yemeni ornament that Muriel bought at our Christmas bazaar. It was the most unusual Christmas tree I've ever seen.

Muriel admires a present for her found under the qat Christmas tree

We put our riyals together and bought a buffalo roast from India – not bad, but then it's been a long time since I have had really good beef. We complemented the roast with a horseradish sauce, frozen broccoli (difficult to find), and mashed potatoes. The potatoes are good here, but no one can find a masher. We used the electric mixer. For dessert June made a key lime pie without the crust but good anyway. Christmas eve we ate four kilos (a little more than 8 pounds) of giant shrimp that we bought in the fish market. The shrimp cost about a $1.00 a pound. We figured the shrimp would have cost us at least $50.00 at home. New Year's Day I tried to cook a several course Italian meal. We began with roasted peppers and roasted tomatoes with basil both marinated in olive oil and garlic. The second course was pasta primavera. I couldn't find any fettuccini so spaghetti had to do. The third course was pieces of chicken cooked with black olives and cauliflower. We also enjoyed wine from the house supply. It wasn't a bad meal or at least I enjoyed it.

Muriel, me, June, and Fran enjoying the patio

After my five weeks of house sitting I put back 6 pounds!! Part of the weight gain was lack of exercise. I hope I've learned my lesson well in preparation for returning to the States. Actually, it seemed good to return to my room and shop in the old dukans. I really missed my fresh kudom (bread). Most of the ex-pat community live in such compounds with high walls and guards at the gates. The only Yemenis on the compounds are maids and workers. But I didn't come to Yemen to live in such luxury. But it sure was a nice vacation.

The maid Fatima is from Somalia. She and her husband came to Yemen to escape the war there, and I enjoyed talking to her about her life in Somalia. On several occasions she broached the subject of Islam and tried to convert me to the true faith. Allah will have no place for me in heaven if I don't convert, she said. An interesting thing she said was that all children are born Muslims as witnessed by the fetal position, the position for prayer in Islam. It's only when we grow up believing in false religions that we become non-Muslims.

Fatima asked me if I could help her get a friend a visa to leave Yemen and go to the USA. She said the friend would pay $300, the going rate for such a favor. I told her that first of all I didn't have any power to help with the visa, and, secondly, it is illegal to charge for the visa. She told me that the Yemeni soldiers who guard all the Western embassies charge people to get near the counsel offices who make the decisions about which refugees will be granted visas. It makes me sick to think that these poor people are victims yet again. Unless they have proper papers the refugees are being rounded up and sent back to Aden to the refugee camps she said. I don't know if that is true. But it could well be. With all Yemen's internal problems, the addition of the Somali refugees makes the situation very difficult.

While I was house sitting, Yahya called to tell me that his mother had died suddenly. He stopped to visit me today. He is understandably very sad, and he has lost another taxi job as the owner no longer needed him. So once again he doesn't have a job. He wants very much to get married before Ramadan. He translated an Arabic proverb for me, loosely translated, meaning, "When your mother is in the kitchen the bread is sweet."

The first semester ended December 31st. We gave our exam the 7th of January. I proctored a huge hallway and five rooms. I wandered from room to room answering questions students had about the exam. In each room there were Yemeni proctors and soldiers with AK-47's patrolling. I don't know why. To shoot cheaters? When I went into one of the rooms one of the Yemeni proctors asked me where I was from in the States. He said "Maybe you can help me go back with you." He paused then said, "You know, you could be my wife." I quickly left the room blushing as I didn't know how to reply to this, my third proposal since I've been here. Or course this proposal was motivated by the desire for a green card.
I spent five days after the exam correcting around 400 exams, not difficult but tedious. Since I finished correcting I have been on vacation. Two of the volunteers I taught with recently returned to the States. So unless changes are made, I will be the only full time American teaching in my department next semester which begins February 6th (we'll see). Ramadan will begin the 23rd or the 24th. Therefore, we will have the month of March off. It is just as well because students don't attend classes regularly during Ramadan, and those who attend have no energy because they are fasting. In other words, the semester will begin for two weeks followed by a five week vacation. It will resume the end of March and continue until sometime in May. At least that is the plan right now.

Muriel and I are planning to travel to Egypt during the Ramadan break. But much will depend on what happens in this part of the World. Right now we have travel restrictions. We were told that the whole Arab World is upset with the USA because of what they perceive as a double standard. They ask, why isn't America concerned about the Palestinian refugees living in camps? Why does America continue to turn a blind eye to the plight of the Palestinians? Why didn't America intervene in Bosnia to save the Muslims there? Anyway, I hope I don't beat this letter home! I've decided I had better see Egypt now while I have a chance. I just hope we will be allowed to go for a couple of weeks. To be this close and fail to visit Egypt would be a shame.

I continue to be involved with the American Women's Group. A couple of weeks ago I went shopping for school uniforms with another woman. Her husband is the military advisor here who was responsible for the safety of the US Marines when they were in Aden. After the hotel bombings in Aden he recommended that the Marines be taken out of Yemen. I'm so glad we decided not to go to Aden for Christmas. We would have been there during the bombings, but we would probably have stayed in cheaper hotels than the ones bombed.

We took the 30 uniforms we bought (15 boys and 15 girls) to the Women's Center where they were distributed to the women who had excelled in literacy classes or had worked hard at the Center sewing or weaving baskets. I also revisited the village where the refugees live recently with Besmire, the president of the organization, and Hyat, the manager. Sad. Our project to help the poor Yemeni children go to school has been funded 50,000 riyals or $1200. This spring we hope to begin registering children for school. We are going to push to educate girls, but not exclude boys. As far as we can tell at this point, a Yemeni child can be sent to school for a year for around 1200 riyals or $30. This includes registration fees, uniforms, and supplies. So our 50,000 riyals should go a long way toward helping a number of Center children.

That's it for today. Until next time,

February 12, 1993

Hi Everyone,

Second semester at the University began last Saturday. At the moment there is chaos. All my classes filled up the first day or two probably because I'm the only native speaker left in the department. I'll be teaching either four or five classes of 60 plus students in each. I have 8 and 10 o'clock classes this semester. I'm glad about this because by May it will be hot in the middle of the day.

The other day I had my first discipline problem. A student just wouldn't shut up. He kept shouting things (his English is pretty good) to the delight of his peers. I asked him several times to be quiet. Finally I had no choice but to ask him to leave the room. Then he became apologetic and asked for a second chance which, of course, I would not grant at this point. His friends then started to plead his case. I really thought he wouldn't leave. I told him that if he didn't leave at once I would leave and not teach the class. He finally left. After class when I was walking home, he drove up and offered me a ride. I was tired and so got in the back seat. He apologized for his behavior all the way to my house and said he wanted to study English with me because he wanted to study with a native speaker. He asked me to chew qat with him. I said someday inshallah (if Allah wills it). I love using that saying in times like this. It saves you from having to say no. Wise guys are the same the World over.

We had an in-service training workshop the beginning of February for TEFL teachers. Because the health problems are so bad here, Peace Corps wants us to use health issues to teach English. It makes sense. But it means designing a new curriculum. Two experts from the States were flown in to run the workshop. We were also encouraged to invite Yemeni teachers to join us. I invited Nora and Eman. They both liked the workshop.

Prices continue to remain high, and it is very difficult to live on the riyals we are given each month. We won't receive our raises until April. Everything is double what it was six months ago. The black market rate is now 47 riyals to the dollar. The bank rate remains the same at 18 riyals to the dollar. The US Embassy recognizes 28 riyals to the dollar. We recently received our IRS statements. For tax purposes the government is converting the riyals we earned into dollars at the 18 rate. In other words, the government is crediting me with a salary of $355 a month, not the $170 a month I actually earned. We wish we could be paid in dollars. It would be so much easier for us. But that's part of the agreement between our government and the Yemen government. So the banks make a tidy little profit on the money the US gives them for us each month.

The hijacking of land rovers continues to be big business here. The man who is second in charge at our Embassy spoke to us last week in order to bring us up to date with the political problems here. As he explained it, the central government is weak because of the in-fighting between the two major political parties, the President's party and the Socialist party from South Yemen. Although they have supposedly mended their fences, their battles have weakened the power of the central government while the power of the tribes is growing stronger. These tribes are now battling each other for power. They hijack cars or kidnap people for ransom. The people who are kidnapped are mainly Westerners because that stirs up the most publicity.

A couple of weeks ago one of the volunteers was at a late night party at the Taj Sheba Hotel with her British boyfriend. When Anne and Rob left the party, they were captured by five or six men with AK-47's on Al-Zubeiry Street. They forced Anne and Rob into a taxi. One of the men held a gun to Anne's head. Rob knocked the gun away and it went off. The noise brought a crowd of people and eventually the police. Fortunately they got away. Rob was banged around a bit and had to have some stitches, but that was the only harm done to them. If the kidnapping attempt had been successful, I would be home now talking to you instead of writing this letter. As you can imagine, we are being very careful about our activities in Sana'a.

There are some anti-American demonstrations caused by our Iraq policy, the perceived double standard regarding the deportation of Palestinians from Israel and the Israeli settlements being built on Palestinian land, and the UN's failure at this point to come to the rescue of Muslims in Bosnia. Yemenis have told me that the United Nations doesn't represent the interest of the whole World, just the West. There does seem, however, to be general approval of the US's role in Somalia.

I am really not afraid for my own safety. Yemenis, for the most part, are friendly and helpful. Of course there is always the random chance of being in the wrong place at the wrong time as is true in any city. We are being careful about where we go and keeping a low profile. We are advised to be in our houses by 10pm. I am always in by 9 o'clock, usually by dark, which is between 6 and 7. The hardest thing about the situation is the uncertainty of it all. Always at the back of my mind is the possibility that we might have to pack up and leave Yemen. I hope the tension quiets down during Ramadan which begins the 22nd or the 23rd of this month and ends after the 'id al-Fitr the 27th of March. As of this writing the postponed elections are scheduled the very end of April, beginning of May. Some people think that this will be the real test of the government's ability to maintain order. There is some concern about the growing popularity of the Islamic Fundamentalist Party. But that party seems to be gaining strength all over the Arab World.

The University will be closed for the five weeks of Ramadan and the 'id al-Fitr following the end of Ramadan. Muriel and I are going to take advantage of the break and travel to Egypt for three weeks. We leave the 1st of March and return the 18th. Our tentative plans are to explore Cairo and the pyramids then go by train to Aswan, travel a bit in that area, take a cruise down the Nile to Luxor, explore the Valley of the Kings, then return to Cairo for shopping, hair styling, and more sight- seeing. Still being considered are Alexandria and a trip into the Sinai. Time and money will determine what we do. The round trip from Sana'a to Cairo is $609. Foreigners have to pay in dollars. It felt so good to use that Master Card again! Khalid, our protector and friend, called Egypt and made a reservation for us at the Garden City House, a pension that someone told us about. Our room is supposed to overlook the Nile. We have been laughing because both of us have known people who have travelled to Egypt and been overcome with the filth. For us it will probably be quite different. We're moving on up! We've heard that you can even buy pork products in Cairo and that there are supermarkets. I am looking forward to going to the American University bookstore.

You probably won't hear from me until after Ramadan as mail is slow then because the services will be drastically cut back. Also, I want to concentrate on my trip and not think about writing letters. I'll write again after I return and tell you about my trip.

Until later,

Camel Crossing

Camel grinding sesame seeds to make oil

March 21, 1993

Greetings Everyone,

I'm back from a great three weeks in Egypt. But I'm exhausted as one always is after a busy trip moving about and visiting temples, ruins, and tombs. Egypt is exotic, but not as exotic as Yemen. To Muriel and me it felt as if we had landed in the Western World. The streets were clean, accommodations quite modern. We laughed silently whenever we talked to one of the token Americans in Egypt. Presumably tourists were scared away because of the recent bombings in Egypt and the bombing of the World Trade Center. The tourists we did talk to always mentioned how dirty the country was. For the life of me, I couldn't see the dirt. Yes, there were slum villages and slum sections of Cairo. However, you can see run down sections in New York, Washington, or Boston. The tourist parts of Cairo seemed clean. Probably it's good that no one will visit me in Sana'a. People would probably be shocked at the dirty streets, dust, and the general living situation that I have grown quite accustomed to.

We stayed in Cairo three days, partly because we wanted to go to the American University bookstore to buy a good travel guide in English, to get our hair styled, and to visit the Egyptian Museum before setting out on our adventure. We also wanted to see the pyramids in Giza before we became jaded. Our hotel, the Garden City, much praised in the "Lonely Planet", lived up to expectations. It is in need of a face lift both inside and out. The beds sagged in the middle, and I always kept one eye scouting for bedbugs which never appeared. The bathroom had no door, but we had our own private toilet and shower with no shower curtain. We don't have shower curtains in our houses so we are used to wet bathroom floors. There was ample hot water available. Our balcony looked out on the Nile. It was a great location, as good as the famous Shepherd's Hotel just down the street. Our room price was better, however. We paid 73 Egyptian pounds a night, the equivalent of $20, $10 each. The price also included breakfast and a choice of lunch or dinner. So what if the breakfast was dried bread and fig jam every morning and the lunch/dinner choice was some type of chicken. It was a great place to stay on a Peace Corps budget.

The hotel guests were fascinating. We got to meet and talk with them at meals which were served family style. All age groups of travelers were there: the young backpackers, the Egyptologists, retired people living in Egypt on pensions, many French and Italians, one Australian woman who had been visiting Egypt for 50 years and prided herself on being the best authority on bus travel, an American woman of indeterminate age who was Blanche right out of "A Street Car Named Desire". We visited with two retired teachers from California who had been traveling in Africa for six months looking at birds. We spent some time touring around the Cairo area with a Lutheran missionary couple who were also traveling in Egypt after being in Tanzania for two years. It was a perfect setting and cast for an Agatha Christie murder mystery--- "Murder on the Nile"????

The first day we tried to go to the bookstore and never made it because we must have had sucker written all over our faces. We started out to walk to the bookstore and were stopped by a "nice young man" who wanted to help us and practice his English. The next thing we knew we were sipping tea in the family papyrus store and being shown our "choices" to buy. After that we were lured into a gold shop where we fought off the pressure to buy gold charms and rings. By the time we escaped, the bookstore was closed. The next day we made it to the bookstore but got trapped again by innocent appearing hustlers. A perfume salesman sold us some "pure Egyptian essence" that turned out to be perfumed olive oil. I was such a willing sucker that I bought both a day and night-time essence. Oh well, olive oil is good for my dry skin and it does smell good. I do have the option of using it on pasta! We soon learned to be wary of anyone who spoke to us. Also, we learned not to accept a favor or help as baksheesh (tips) was always demanded for the service. We were like country Yemenis come to Babylon. In Yemen you don't tip so it was a real cultural shock for us. We didn't like the big bazaar Khan Kalili because we found it to be a tourist trap. Our suq in Sana'a is authentic and you can look at things without being hassled.

There were so few tourists in Egypt because of the terrorist threats that there never were any lines anywhere, and all the hotels were almost empty. Our hotel was close to the café that was bombed and to the Egyptian museum where a tourist bus had a bomb planted under it. It was a great time to travel cheaply. After living in Yemen for a year and a half, what's another bomb? Perhaps it was safer in Cairo than in New York in light of the bombing at the New York Trade Center. We just marched right up to the pyramids and had most of the space around them to ourselves. We heard that usually the area is crawling with tourists. Yes, the pyramids are massive. It was hard for me to believe that I was actually there touching and looking at them. We actually visited them twice. The second time we stopped there on the way to Saqqara to see the Step Pyramid. Muriel and I sat, drank tea, and just looked at them. The Egyptian Museum is very impressive. I was especially thrilled to see the King Tut rooms. It was a good introduction to Egyptian history.

Muriel at the Giza Pyramids　　*I'm sitting on one of the Pyramids.*

We left by train for Aswan on March 4th. We travelled first class on the day train because we wanted to see the countryside. It cost $15 for the 15 hour trip. What an incredible journey through the Nile valley so green and lush: antique farming, villages, and farmers in the fields of sugar cane and something that looked like clover, donkeys, camels, water buffaloes pulling handmade plows juxtaposed to modern tractors, women and girls washing dishes and laundry in the muddy river that paralleled the railroad track. We talked with two American women on the train who had stayed at our hotel in Cairo, although we didn't see them there. Christine, in her twenties, was from Boston and a TWA employee. Barbara, a bank teller in her 40's, was from Washington State who had saved her money for three years so that she could make a six week trip to Egypt. Barbara had left her husband and two teenage daughters at home to make the trip which had been a life time dream. We traveled with Barbara for a week. Christine had to return to Boston.

In Aswan we had a hotel with a balcony view of the Nile. We took a felucca trip on the Nile, stopping at several islands to walk around including Philae Island with a wonderfully preserved temple, Elphantine Island with a Nubian village and Kitchener's island with a lush botanical garden.

One morning we set out at 4am on a three hour ride through the desert in a taxi to Abu Simbel, now on Lake Nasser only 40 kilometers from the Sudan border. It was freezing cold before the sun came up. We stopped to take pictures of the sunrise. Abu Simbel is amazing. But to me one of the most amazing things is to realize that the statues of Ramses and his Queen were taken apart and reassembled in this new spot because the water from the new dam now covers their original site. Our trip back to Aswan was hot as the sun beat into the taxi windows. We saw an honest to goodness herd of camels in the desert.

House painted to show resident had visited Mecca

King Ramses and Queen

From Aswan we traveled by taxi to the Kom Ombo and Edfu temples on the way to Luxor. We had planned to travel by felucca, but you needed a sleeping bag for an overnight trip. The steamer was tempting, but we wanted to have the time to travel in the Sinai. Our traveling group now included two Chinese girls who were studying in Germany and four young Dutch men. We had a great time with them all. Our minivan driver stopped for a tea break. He literally drove into the shabby open sided café. We decided that this "drive-in" restaurant beat any drive-in place at home! In Luxor we met Muhammad, our 20 year old guide who asked me to marry him. Do you suppose he was after a green card? The best thing about Luxor was the Karnak Temple. It's massive and inspiring. It contains a huge forest of columns still in excellent shape. The reliefs were more rounded and lively than I had been led to think from the pictures I'd seen. We went to a sound and light show at Karnak that we loved. We explored the Luxor temple and saw the empty pedestal where the obelisk that Napoleon took back to France with him used to stand. Now it stands in Place de la Concorde in Paris. In Cairo there is a clock that the French later gave Egypt in apology for "taking" the obelisk. However, the clock has never worked! Of course, we visited the Valley of the Kings. I found this part of the trip disappointing as the tombs looked pretty modern and sterile. But to be fair, I was "tombed" out at this point and have decided I don't want to spend eternity in such a place.

Relief in Karnak Temple

Muriel embracing column

In front of the Sphinx

Inside Karnak Temple

From Luxor we traveled in a very crowded bus with people standing in the aisles for four hours to Hurghada on the coast of the Red Sea. We slept in a hotel there and then got up to take the early morning ferry ride to Sham el Sheikh on the tip of the Sinai. The 5 hour ferry ride was great, albeit a little rough at times. In Sham el Sheikh we caught a bus to Na'ama Bay, a few miles away. We gasped in wonder because we had arrived in a Florida resort. Malls, plush hotels and gourmet restaurants. Muriel and I just wandered around in amazement. Our hotel room that we shared with Barbara was expensive, $28 apiece, but it was worth it. We ate calamari and drank red wine. What a treat. For dessert we had chocolate sundaes. It was real ice cream.

The next day we traveled by private taxi for three hours (180 pounds, $54. dollars split three ways) to St Catherine's Monastery at the foot of Mt. Sinai. We stayed in a hostel there and ate in the common dining room. We rode camels part way up Mr. Sinai. No we didn't climb to the top in the night to watch the sunrise. It was too cold.

The next day we explored the 4th Century A.D. Greek Orthodox Monastery and saw the burning bush of Moses fame. We didn't break any commandants while we were in this brown, quiet, cold, austere, barren place that looked as if it must have been where the World began or where it will end. We missed the Cairo bus so Muriel and I said good-bye to Barbara who was traveling to Israel and decided to hire a taxi for $60 to drive us the six hours through the Sinai, and over the Suez Canal to Cairo. In Cairo we finished touring the city: Islamic Cairo, Old Cairo, and Coptic Cairo. We talked with the old gang at the Garden City Hotel and shopped. The hustlers left us alone as I guess the sucker look no longer adorned our faces. A life time dream was fulfilled in this 18 day trip to Egypt. I'm glad I did it now because this whole part of the World is so unstable you don't know what will happen next. I'm hoping that when I leave Yemen next February that I'll be able to visit Jordan and Syria on my way to Turkey.

Until Next Time,

Mt Sinai

Camel ride for Muriel and me

St. Catherine's Monastery

Nubian sailor

Drive-in restaurant on the way to Luxor

April 19, 1993

Hi Everyone,

It's cold and rainy in Sana'a!! It's been this way for two weeks now and enough is enough. I walk to the University dodging mud and mud puddles. My shoes are caked with mud every day. It's especially nasty walking in the dirt roads that sometimes cannot be avoided. At home I huddle in my sweat suit and try to keep warm. I'm told that it's very unusual weather for Sana'a. Bring back the sun!

Since I returned from Egypt not much has happened here, just my usual schedule at the University. Perhaps you can imagine how dirty the building must be with students and teachers tracking in mud. Sometimes the halls are swept, but the rooms aren't. Yesterday, I couldn't stand it anymore. I borrowed a broom from one of the custodians in order to sweep out my room. The same day a bird had the audacity to fly through my room which really gave me a start. The students were amused by my little scream. The building I teach in will be closed the 21st of May, we're told, so that the custodial staff can prepare the building for exams. DON'T ASK ME WHAT THEY DO!! We don't know if that means classes will stop then or not. At any rate, they will probably end at the end of May. The 'id al-Adha that is celebrated two months after the end of Ramadan begins on May 27 so classes will probably be finished by that time.
I think I wrote that we met a TWA employee from Boston when we were traveling in Egypt. Two days before Easter Muriel got a call from Yemenia Airlines informing us that a package was at the airport for us. I guess airlines extend this courtesy to send packages through customs, like a diplomatic pouch, to their employees and to employees of other airlines. Christine sent us a big box of goodies including: two hams, Easter baskets, package mixes, Girl Scout cookies, canned clams, cookies, candy, Cape Cod potato chips, tuna fish, and after dinner mints. It was an overwhelming and unexpected gift. I have had a great time eating chocolate and more chocolate. We had a great Easter dinner.

I don't remember if I've written about how we cook meals on our three burner gas table-top stove. It's connected to a gas tank, called butagas, such as we use for gas grills at home. Anyway, we have learned to bake without an oven. We put an empty tuna fish can in the bottom of a big pot and place a small pot with whatever we want to bake in the big pot on top of the tuna can. Then if the gas is turned low, we can bake. In this fashion June and I prepared Easter dinner. Of course, we had to prepare some things the day before because of the limited cooking space and pots. June baked delicious brownies in this fashion, and I went to the suq and bought a giant cabbage (they only sell giant cabbages here) that was so heavy I had to transport it home in a taxi to make coleslaw. Oh for a good food processor or at least a hand held shredder. Fortunately I did bring a sharp knife with me to Yemen. I swear there isn't a sharp knife to be bought in Yemen! On Easter we cooked the rest of the meal—baked ham with cloves and a Dijon mustard sauce, cauliflower with cheese sauce, baked sweet potatoes with a sauce (I baked a regular one for myself). For dessert we ate the brownies and shared the candy from our Easter baskets with our PCV friends. It was a great meal. The ham sandwiches the next day were delicious.

Last Friday I made clams linguine for Artis, Muriel and me. Clams are not available here, not even canned ones. I even made a pretty good garlic bread, and Artis came up with a passable white wine. I've perfected a tasty vinaigrette to put on the Clorox washed vegetables. We have to soak our raw vegetables and fruit in boiled water that has cooled and a few drops of Clorox for 25 minutes. Then we rinse them well before eating. Christine also sent us a package of dried onion soup that I made a dip with. Sour cream is unavailable so we use yogurt which is very good in Yemen. Since large bags of potato chips are nonexistent, we buy 20 of the small bags, open them and place them in a serving bowl.

Rose, the woman who fell at the Ma'rib Dam, is back with us. She has nearly recovered from her accident, but she does have a noticeable limp. She says that walking up and down hills in Hajja, where she is stationed, will be good therapy. Muriel and I went to Hajja to visit her soon after our return from Egypt because Rose returned while we were out of the country, and we wanted to see her. While we were in Hajja we made some banana and raisin wine (the only available fruit in the suq). Rose brought some wine making kits back with her. The wine won't be ready until sometime this summer. Probably it will be too sweet. But it will be wine at least as good as Boone's Farm. Grape season will be here soon so we hope to make some grape wine.

I had lunch the other day at the home of my Sudanese friend Huda. Her Dutch husband had made some delicious dry-explodes-in-your-mouth-and-then-disappears red wine. He also has made some beer that is supposed to be good. They promised me they would invite me back to sample once the beer is bottled.

The big news in Yemen is the approaching elections April 27th. There are all kinds of rumors of buying votes and other forms of corruption. The president, Ali Abdullah Saleh, is supposedly in his village now under the protection of his private army. The Socialist vice president from the South has gone home to muster support. Candidates will be elected to parliament, and the parliament will choose the president. The Yemenis I talk to say Ali Abdullah Saleh will again be president, but many people are unhappy with him.

All appears to be going smoothly even though several government employees are having trouble collecting their salaries: teachers, soldiers, garbage men, and students who are studying to be teachers. Prices are expected to rise after the elections, the dollar to jump even higher. Unemployment continues to be high.

Peace Corps is moving us to al-Hudayda for five days during the elections. I'm sure from all reports that there will be no major problems, but Sana'a is where problems will probably erupt if any occur. Where else could I have a job where I would be forced to take a five-day vacation at the sea? Peace Corps will pay for our hotel (El Bourg where I stayed last summer with the wonderful covered porch that I've written about), breakfast and lunch and give us a per diem with which we have to buy dinner. Bring on the great blackened fish! Our mornings will be spent attending a mandatory first aid training course. The afternoon will be free. Probably we will spend the heat of the day resting and playing cribbage and bridge. In the late afternoon we will swim in the Red Sea. The University will be closed during this time period as well. If all is well we will return to Sana'a or wherever volunteers are stationed the 29th of April.

So that's all for now folks. I hope to hear from you all soon. Take a good whiff of the lilacs when they bloom for me.

Until Next Time,

May 29, 1993

Greetings One and All,

How's the lilac season? I expect it is at its height as I write this. I certainly miss the blooming of spring. In Sana'a it just gets hotter. The seasonal changes are more subtle. Rainy season appears to be over now, but the crops should be good as there was abundant rain during April and much of May. Although it is getting hotter, the nights still cool off. As long as you stay inside during the hot part of the day, it's not bad.

Classes for me at the University ended a week ago. As expected, the building I teach in closed to get ready for exams. The Yemenis I teach with and I are making up the exam on my computer for the expected 2000 students who might take it. We don't know how many for sure as some students never register for class. They just take the final. If they pass the final, they get credit for the course. We have to run off the tests on an old mimeograph machine. The exam will be given, we think, the 21st of June. Everything is always subject to change. The end of June, beginning of July will be spent correcting the exams. Even though I've finished teaching for the semester, it will be another month before I'm free from the University.

This past week I attended a three-day Peace Corps SPA (small projects assistance) workshop where we learned about small projects that we might wish to do. The workshop taught us how to get money and write proposals. For a specific project we can receive up to $10,000 from USAID. Anne and I want to try to write a proposal for the Women's Center that will be rewarded with grant money. We will have to talk with the board of directors of the Center. If we can come up with a workable project, it will be a good summer project.

Also, this summer, June 20th through August 20th, I will be housesitting for a young couple who teach at the American International School in Sana'a. They're going to return to Minnesota for the summer. Their house isn't as luxurious as the one I stayed in at Christmas, but it is more luxurious than where I live. It has a washing machine, TV and VCR, a real stove with an oven, plus Western style furniture—couches, chairs, a bed, and a dining room table. Outside there are flowers and a grape arbor that I can use the grapes from to make wine while I'm staying there. Two rabbits wander about the garden eating weeds. They had two chickens but agreed to get rid of them if I'd housesit. The house is near the Peace Corps office and about a mile from my new apartment that I recently moved into. So the location is convenient. They understand that I will make occasional overnight trips in Yemen and also understand that friends will visit me at the house. They also said they are willing to carry a suitcase back to the States for me and send it to my brother with UPS. I will be able to get some things I've collected back to the States which is safer than mailing it from here.

My new apartment is near the Old University. There are five apartments in the building, one on each floor, all filled with Peace Corps people. Our apartment is on the first floor, one floor above the ground floor. My bedroom looks out on busy Kuwait St. and the University. We have a big hallway, small kitchen and bath, and a good sized mafraj. Anne's room is similar to mine. I have a little balcony that I can go out onto through my bedroom window which is like a small version of French windows. We have a clothes line there to hang out our laundry. It is more convenient to the University and public transportation. Also, it's nice to live in a house with other Americans and be able to wander around inside the building in shorts and tee shirts. My friends Muriel and June live two floors up.

I had no plans to move, but Anne, a young teacher in Sana'a who is part of my original group, lost her roommate who got married and left Yemen. Anne couldn't afford to keep the apartment on her own. She asked me to move in with her. I agreed as long as I didn't create a financial hardship for my former roommates. I took only my personal things out of the house, and when we leave next year we will settle up with our household stuff. I like living in my new apartment. Anne is easy to get along with and away a lot with her British boyfriend. So I have the apartment to myself a lot. Artis and my ex-pat friend Pipette helped me move. Pipette has a land cruiser which made the move easy. I was surprised, though, with how much stuff I've accumulated since I've been in Yemen.

My new bedroom

Apartment building with PCV's on balconies

We recently lost two more from our original group of volunteers. There are only eight of us left here from the original 16. Fifty percent is a high dropout rate, but life here, although stimulating and rewarding, is difficult at times. It's particularly hard for the young women who are midwives in villages. It's lonely and the social restrictions are difficult for them to handle. Living in Sana'a is much easier. I don't know if I could stay in Yemen if I lived in a village by myself.

Yesterday I went to Ton and Huda's house for a barbeque. The fresh tuna was so delicious grilled. We also drank Ton's homemade beer and wine. It was so pleasant sitting under a shade tree in their garden eating a slowly paced meal and talking. Ton is here working for Dutch Development, trying to solve Yemen's water problem. Another dinner guest was Joseph who also works for Dutch Development. It was such a pleasure to spend the day with interesting people. On June 7th Karin, an Indian woman whose husband is the manager of the Sheraton Hotel in Sana'a, has asked Huda and me to join her for lunch at the Sheraton. I really enjoy jumping about in my life here, sitting on the floor eating with my fingers in Yemeni homes to trying to remember how to manipulate silverware in ex-pats' homes or hotels.

The 'id al-Adha will start here on Monday. People travel to their ancestral villages to celebrate this holiday. They also sacrifice lambs or goats and give some of the meat to poor people. Remember I wrote about the short happy life of poor Nick a year ago?

Eric is in town now staying with me. Anne is traveling so the apartment is mine to share with other volunteers who are in town. On the 31st of May, Muriel and I are planning to go back to Ibb with Eric for a couple of days to visit his site. Ibb is so green and beautiful. Khalid has invited Muriel and me to go to Manakha, his ancestral village in the Haraz Mountains west of Sana'a, sometime in July. We also want to visit Rose in Hajja this summer if she is still there. She is having a lot of trouble with her leg that was broken in Ma'rib. The end of August, after my house sitting job, I am planning to go to Tanzania and Kenya for a couple of weeks to go on safari, see Mt. Kilimanjaro, visit Nairobi, the Rift Valley and Zanzibar. It should be an interesting summer with a little variety. This coming fall Peace Corps will celebrate its 20th anniversary in Yemen. All kinds of events are being planned. Before I know it, I will be leaving Yemen and flying home. Two years is such a short time.

That brings you up to date with my life. What's happening in yours?

Bye for Now,

June 19, 1993

Hi Everyone,

June 1st Muriel and I went to Ibb by group Taxi to visit Eric. I was in Ibb last summer for a couple of days, and it was great to return to this lush area and be shown around by someone who knows the area. Because of the rains, the mountainsides and terraces were a particularly vivid green.

Two of Eric's students walked us through the old city of Ibb that is perched on top of a hill with narrow stone streets, tall stone houses, and small dukans along the twisted way. One of the boys guiding us was born in this section of the town and pointed out the ancestral homes where his grandfather kept his two wives.

After a long walking tour we went to visit an Indian professor, Dr. Shama, Eric has befriended. As we sipped lukewarm imitation orange juice, Dr. Shama lectured us on Hindu and Indian philosophy. Very entertaining and thought provoking. He is a charming man. A couple of months ago he published his first book in India and promised to bring copies back from India when he returns from summer vacation.

The next day we went by taxi to Bardain, a village on top of a mountain overlooking Ibb. It was a steep mountain climb. Our taxi stalled, and the driver couldn't get the car started again. We were in one of the few dips in an otherwise steep trail. He had another taxi pull us backward down the mountain so that he could jump start the car. Now let me tell you, that was a thrill! But it worked and we chugged our way to the top.

We went in search of the sheik of the village whom Eric knows. Sheik Amien was delighted to see us, and proudly walked us through his village and commandeered a car to take us to another village close by. He took us into one house that was filled with men. We walked into the mafraj and were told to sit near what appeared to be a sick old man sitting with blankets wrapped around him. We soon discovered he was a young man, probably in his early thirties. His lips and tongue were white! I have never seen anything like it. He spoke with a perfect American accent. He had returned to Yemen from New York for the 'id al-Adha celebration, he told us, and bad food had made him sick. He looked as if he had been sick for a long time and had the look of death. My eyes kept focusing on his white lips and tongue. I couldn't help it. I'm sure he had AIDS. When Sheik Amien said it was time to go he almost cried, begging us to stay and eat lunch with him. I have eaten all kinds of questionable food in this country, but I couldn't eat or drink there. Eric and the Sheik promised to return the following Friday to visit him. I was relieved when we went to Sheik Amien's house for a traditional Yemeni lunch of salta, rice, boiled lamb, bread, bananas and tea. We sat cross legged on the floor of the mafraj eating out of the same dish, using our bread and fingers to pick up food. Of course, his wife, who had prepared the lunch, couldn't eat with us because Eric was there. The oldest son who was about 18 brought the food from the kitchen and joined us for lunch. After lunch Sheik Amien played rock and roll cassettes. He told us that he had been a professional dancer in London in the 1950's and that he had once danced with Chubby Checker's band. Let me tell you it was a bizarre experience being in a Yemeni house on a remote mountain top watching a Yemeni man dressed in a zenna and jambiya twisting to the sound of "Let's Twist Again". I tried to take a picture when Muriel joined him, but he wouldn't let me.

Eric, Sheik Amien, and Muriel   *Muriel with children in Ibb*

That evening we visited some Southern Baptist missionaries Eric knows who run a hospital in Jibla. We went to a prayer meeting with them. This was another strange experience being with this fundamentalist Christian group at a prayer meeting smack dab in the middle of fundamentalist, Islamic Yemen. The missionaries are allowed to practice their religion because they give medical care to Yemenis, but they aren't allowed to proselytize in Yemen.

The next day, Dr. Martha, a missionary doctor, drove us and another woman down the mountain into the wadi and what felt like an African jungle. We drove through streams; bamboo went rat-tat-tat against the land rover. We felt as if we were driving in the wild kingdom. She drove to a very remote area that she visits periodically to offer medical attention to the few people in the area. She is obviously a heroine to the people living there. It was heartwarming to see the kind, gentle way she offered the only medical attention the people in this area receive. One man came to fetch her to visit his sick wife. After she had helped her, we stopped beside a stream to watch a man Dr. Martha had befriended make a big basket (the kind we would use as a laundry basket at home).

Man making basket

The road we drove on with Dr. Martha

Dr. Martha with the children

His wife showed Dr. Martha a neighbor's child who was in obvious pain. Dr. Martha said the baby had a hernia in his belly button. She held the baby's stomach and massaged it until the pain went away. This was an inspiring trip with this remarkable woman. I felt as if I were in a novel traveling about with a woman missionary doctor in the deepest jungle. But, yes, I was. It wasn't pretend.

The 15th of June Khalid took Muriel and me to Manakha, 90 km west of Sana'a. This is Khalid's ancestral homeland, and he wanted us to see it. We booked into a Yemeni style hotel. Muriel and I shared a large mafraj with the most magnificent mountain scenery I have ever looked out on from a hotel room. Because the room was essentially a mafraj, it was filled with windows. We could see mountains towering above us and smaller peaks below us. Manakha is 2200 meters above sea level. The old city of Manakha surrounded the hotel. I felt like Heidi just arrived at grandfather's house. At night we unrolled the mattresses provided and put them on the mafraj cushions. We had brought our own sheets, fortunately, as this was a NO SHEET hotel. Our meals were served in this room. Khalid joined us then. At night we played dominoes.

Khalid and Muriel in Manakha

Khalid and me in the mafraj

Muriel and Khalid sharing a meal in the mafraj in our hotel

The day we arrived in Manakha, Khalid said we should make the half hour climb to his village of Khahil. It wasn't a bad climb, he said. Well, it took us an hour and a half! It was very steep in places and very hot climbing. Khalid kept finding shortcuts for us that became genuine rock climbing exercises. A couple of times he had to take off his shawl (he was climbing in his zenna, suit jacket, jambiya, and loafers) to pull Muriel and me up over difficult parts. He had told us that we didn't need to bring water as it was a short climb and that we could buy water at a dukan on top of the mountain. Well, you guessed it. When we arived on the mountain top with our tongues hanging out, the dukan was closed because the owner had gone to Sana'a to attend a wedding. We went to Khalid's ancestral home where two old women kindly served us tea. We watched thirstily as Khalid drank the water we didn't dare to drink as it wasn't boiled water. I came close to drinking it, but good sense prevailed. We sucked on some grape sized peaches on the way down to put moisture in our mouths. We were exhausted. Khalid seems to have no idea of our ages. At one point he said his mother never returned to her village as it was difficult for a woman to make the trip up the mountain. What are we? I'm sure his mother must be younger than we are! But anyway, we took his comment as a compliment.

Muriel and Khalid resting on the mountain top

The next day Khalid took us on an easy walk, he assured us, to the coffee bean fields outside of Manakha. We started off at 8am with one liter of water. After walking in a rough road for at least four miles, we arrived at the coffee bean fields. We visited with the men, women, and children working the fields, scaled ten feet high stone walls going from field to field and then continued on our way in search of a village Khalid wanted to show us. Finally, Muriel and I were exhausted and the water was gone. The sun was very intense, and we needed water. We found a shade tree and sent Khalid to the next village to find water. Three young farmers came by to share our shade tree and visit. They played a game they called bayt (house) that appeared to be a crude form of the game monopoly.

An hour later, Khalid returned after walking to three villages in search of bottled water. There was none as the economy is so poor in the area no one could afford bottled water. He found us some water that had been boiled for tea. Although I questioned it silently, I was too thirsty to resist. We began the long trek back to the hotel in the hottest part of the day. Khalid had wanted us to continue on our journey, but we refused to go any farther knowing we would have to walk back. We got back to Manakha about 2pm VERY THIRSTY. We bought three ice cold liters of water and engulfed them. It was an eventful two days of walking, trekking through Yemeni mountains. I was delighted to see Khalid's village as he is so proud of its history and beauty. It was built on a mountain peak as many villages in Yemen are for security reasons.

Khalid and me in the coffee fields.

Muriel and Khalid in Manakha

Two nights ago I went to a cocktail buffet party at Pipette and Joe's house. I should say, a villa. The garden party was catered by one of the best hotels in Sana'a. Over a hundred ex-pats from several countries enjoyed good food and an open bar. Tomorrow I move into my summer house I am housesitting. It's not as outstanding as the Christmas house but nothing to sneeze at either. I'll be living there until around August 20th.

That's all for now,

July 13, 1993

Happy Summer Everyone,

It's already the middle of summer. I can't believe how quickly time is passing. However, summer only began officially for me a few days ago when we were dismissed from the University. We will have periodic meetings as all the volunteers at the University are being transferred to the English Education Department where I teach. At this point I have no idea what I will be teaching in the fall.

Thirty-eight new volunteers arrived in Yemen a few days ago. Most of them are health volunteers, and they come from diverse backgrounds and sections of the States. The age range is also big, except that most of them do appear younger than the last group. They will not go through training in Sana'a as the last two groups have. Instead, they will live and train in Ta'zz, about 4 to 5 hours south of here. We won't see that much of them because of the distance, but most of us will make at least one trip there to meet them. At the moment there is a cholera outbreak in Ta'zz which means we must be careful about eating and drinking in restaurants.

I'll go to Ta'zz the first part of August with my roommate Anne to do a WID (women in development) workshop for the new PCV's. Anne and I are really involved with women's projects, and we are going to try to get more volunteers involved with these projects. Also, we will try to give them a more realistic picture of women's lives here than we received. Basically, we had the impression that all Yemeni women lived closed lives in their homes cooking and having babies with no other choices available to them. While this is true for the majority of Yemeni women, it is far from the accurate picture. There are a growing number of finely educated and politically active women who are striving to improve their lives and the lives of other women.

My friend Elham is an example of a liberated Yemeni woman. She is a divorced mother of two elementary aged sons. She lives alone with them and teaches English. Last spring she courageously fought the reactionary administration at her school to try to win better salaries for her Yemeni colleagues. The school was on strike for at least six months. Finally, they won their battle. Elham has received a Fulbright scholarship and will study at the University of Arizona for the next two years. But she has to leave her two sons in Yemen with their father, not an easy decision for her to make. There are many examples of such courageous women. We want the new volunteers to be aware of this fact early on.

I am enjoying my house sitting job very much. It is a comfortable house with a nice garden. I am actually looking after roses again. We have had several bridge parties in the garden. We eat lunch and then move the dining room table outside under the grape arbor to play cards. I am also enjoying the video player. There is a local video store where we rent pirated videos (no copyright laws here) of some recent USA films. "The Unforgiven" won the best picture recently, didn't it? Of course the videos are not as sharp as they should be because they were probably recorded right from the big screen in a theater. The videos here are for European video machines, not American ones.

Eric is in town before he leaves on a six week trip to East Africa. He is staying with me in the house. Artis is also a frequent visitor as well as the Golden Girls. Tonight we are going to have a BLT sandwich party. Michael, a PCV who was in Germany recently, brought back some German bacon which we are going to fry. We will wash the sandwiches down with mushmushkila (no problem). Mushmushkila is the name we gave the banana and raison wine that Rose, Muriel, and I made in Hajja this past spring.

Last week I went to Al-Bathia in southeast Yemen on a site visit with two health volunteers. Peace Corps is thinking of putting two of the new health volunteers in the mother child clinic there. Our job was to check out the place and see what the clinic is like as well as prospective living conditions for volunteers. Obviously, I couldn't contribute much as I am not knowledgeable about health clinics, but I wouldn't want to have a hangnail removed there! It was very unsanitary, dusty, and had dirty sheets on the examination table. There were unsterilized instruments lying about. The town itself was very dusty and uninspiring, on the whole a mean place to live. I'm so thankful to be living in Sana'a.

We made the trip to Al-Bathia by taxi, and on the way we ran literally into locusts that are ravaging Yemen's crops. I had never seen locusts until I came to Yemen. They are huge, three to four times the size of grasshoppers. It was like having small birds splat on the windshield. Very unnerving. A student brought me a locust in May. I thought it was a toy battery powered grasshopper that he had brought to scare me. Then I discovered it was real! The Yemenis love to eat them. The joke is that the locusts eat all the vegetation in Africa, but when they come to Yemen the Yemenis eat the locusts. Anyway, the joke is not so funny anymore. The invasion of locusts has become a monumental problem that is being fought by the UN. Experts are being flown in from around the world to try to find a way to get rid of the locusts.

I went to a reception for Al and Sharon Firman (the couple I house sat for at Christmas) who are returning to the States. Al is the director of FAO (Food and Agriculture Organization, a division of the UN) in Yemen. It has been his office's job to fight this plague. He said that the locusts got out of control because Yemenis failed to report the invasion for a week as they were too busy trying to catch them to eat. They came in through the desert in Saudi Arabia. The experts are also running into problems trying to spray because the bee keepers are afraid of losing their bees. According to the Yemen Times one fifth of the country is covered with locusts, and it is feared that the crop loss with be great. We haven't seen too many of them in Sana'a, but we ran into a swarm on the way to Al-Bathia.

I went to visit Sharon Firman before they moved from the apartment to go back to the States. She gave me six diet cokes, a stick of pepperoni, and a bottle of Heinz ketchup, all very precious items. She is going to give me her toaster oven when they leave in a couple of weeks.

The American Embassy put on a big July 4th picnic for the American community. They served hotdogs, hamburgers, salads, and beer. There was live music as well. PCV's didn't have to pay for tickets to attend.

Rose of the Ma'rib incident is going back home as her leg is bothering her, and she is in a lot of pain. Perhaps she will have to have surgery. She is mailing this letter to you. We are sad to have her go.

Until my next letter,

A truck load of Yemeni men going to a party? To work?

Man praying

Playing Bridge under a grape arbor

Rose, Gladys, June and me enjoying house sitting

Men going to work? to a party?

August 8, 1993

Greetings Everyone,

So, you're having a hot summer. The end of July was pretty beastly here as well, but fortunately the weather pattern has shifted, and we're in the beginning of another rainy season. It was so dry at the end of July that my nose was irritated by the sand swirling about in the wind, altogether unpleasant. Flu is still making its rounds or a sickness with flu-like symptoms. I was sick for over a week at the end of July: allergy like nose problems, headache, sinus blockage, upset stomach, diarrhea, and fever. I had no energy for a long time, but now I'm my old self.

Last week Anne and I spent a couple of days in Ta'izz at the training site for the new volunteers. We did a WID presentation for them, mainly talking about our secondary projects and what other volunteers are doing for their projects. Anne and I volunteer at the Women's Center for our secondary project. It was fun to meet and talk with the new PCV's. One of the new volunteers is from Rutland, VT, and a recent UVM graduate. Their training facilities are more modern than our training site, but both Anne and I agreed that we feel fortunate to have trained in the Old City of Sana'a. We were dumped immediately into the heart of Yemen. One of the positive results is that I feel very comfortable wandering around the Old City. It's home. Our trip to Ta'izz was an adventure in the taxi. In the mountainous area of Ibb we ran into a bad hail storm. Our driver finally decided it was prudent to stop to let the storm pass. When we started up the mountain again we ran into fast flowing rivers and two rock slides. At home the road would have been closed, but we just drove around the rock piles and through the rivers. Both of us were relieved to arrive in Ta'izz unscratched.

My friend Huda had a women's party recently with dinner and soft drinks. There were about 20 women there from Yemen, Sudan, Iraq, India, Ethiopia, Holland and me, the lone American. There were in fact only four Westerners there. As I have written before, in Yemen men and women do not socialize together except in families. Usually I find these parties pretty dull. The women really dress up, bright dresses, much make-up and big hair. They dance quite erotically to Yemeni Music, the whine of which becomes tedious to a Westerner's ear. Even if English is spoken, the conversation is often dull.

Huda's party was an exception. All the women there were bright, informed, educated, and the conversation sparkled. The only low point for me was when I found out that the stimulating woman I was sitting next to was from Iraq. We were bombing Iraq at the time. We, of course, didn't discuss the issue, and Huda apologized later for not warning me that an Iraqi woman was present. It made me feel sad that Huda thought I had to be apologized to. I'm not sure what I think politically about the Iraq situation, but I know what I feel as a human being. Many of the Iraqi people living in Yemen do not support their leader, but they have friends and families in Iraq who live in fear of the next US bomb. It does not make me feel proud. I wish every American had to meet the people I know face to face here in Yemen. Sometimes Yemenis will ask why are Arabs always referred to as terrorists and fundamentalists in the US press. Not all Arabs are violent American haters, they point out. Khalid for instance is a Shia'a. No one could be more reasonable and kind. I would trust him with my life. We have a long way to go to understand each other, the East and the West. We must understand that there is a lot of resentment and distrust of Westerners in this part of the World still because of colonialism. Many Arabs think that our main reason for being here now is to take away the oil. Anyway, Huda's party was a lot of fun. I really enjoyed being part of such an international group.

I have been involved with a very interesting project this summer that I learned about from Karin Palmer, the Indian woman whose husband is the manager of the Sheraton Hotel. There is a major problem here with the Somali refugees. They need food, medical care, housing and jobs. We don't see many of them in Sana'a because most of them are detained in the South in camps near Aden. But there is misunderstanding and resentment on the part of some Yemenis toward them. So the UNHCR (the UN High Commission for Refugees) wants stories written for Yemeni school children to educate them about the problems of the refugees and to raise their compassion and sensitivity to this problem. Karin was asked to take over the project, and she asked me to help. Two other women are also on the committee; Theresa, an American woman I know from the American Women's Group who fled Cuba as a child when Castro came to power, and Layla, a British/Yemeni woman (father Yemeni, mother British) who teaches at the University. The other two members are men, a Yemeni artist and an Iraqi artist married to the stimulating woman I met at Huda's party. We decided to write three children's stories to raise awareness of the plight of the Somali refugees. The first story will be for 7 to 9 year olds, the second for 10 to 12 year olds, and the third for 13 to 16 year olds. The first story will mainly be a picture book with captions; the second story will contain more writing but will have several illustrations. The third book is a story without illustrations. We're going to write the stories in English and then have them translated into Arabic.

I wrote the story for the oldest group. I was actually quite pleased with how it turned out, and I had fun setting the story in the Old City. It was a little Pollyannaish, but our purpose was not to write great literature but to change attitudes about refugees. Anyway, when I read the story to the group, they all said it was a good story that met our humanistic goals. The only problem was that the heroine in the story is an American girl in shashaf (veiled) wandering around the Old City. I was shocked and asked why they thought that was true. They said the girl thinks like an American. I asked how an American thinks. I was told that Americans think very directly and freely. A Yemeni girl doesn't have the romantic thoughts a Westerner has, and certainly she doesn't understand freedom the same way an American does. I am still reeling from this information. I had been so conscientious about trying to respect cultural mores which I was very careful about in the story. But I can't get in the Yemeni head.

My thinking process is different by virtue of my nationality. I felt so locked into a little box, finally recognizing what they said is true. I suppose all this is obvious, but it is a new idea to me and the ramifications of it are endless. Certainly it makes it easier to accept what we think of strange behavior in someone from a different culture. We had a great conversation about these differences in the thinking process that people from different cultures have. Layla teaches writing in the master's program at the University and is doing her dissertation for her PHD on why it is difficult for Arabic speakers to write well in English. She plans to assign her students to write a story with the same theme as mine and see how the heroine turns out. So, anyway, my story with modifications as well as the other two will be translated and printed by UNHCR and distributed to children in Yemeni public schools this fall. We also have to write a teachers' guide with suggested activities. Yemeni artists will illustrate the books. Artists are pretty much marginalized here, so Karin and I were talking about trying to do something to promote Yemeni artists. But too soon it will be time for me to go home to take on this project.

Some of you have been asking me about my plans after January, 1994. I don't know. I know that even though I have enjoyed my time in Yemen and have learned a lot, I want to go home. It's time. I must and want to find a job immediately as I will be broke (so what's new?). As a returned Peace Corp Volunteer I will have a special classification competing for Federal jobs that I am qualified for. This classification will be good for a year. Peace Corps maintains a job search office in Washington. I expect I'll go there to see what I can find. I do want a job where I will earn some real money for a change. I know the job market is tough. I don't want to teach in a traditional classroom. What I have confirmed about myself is that I like adventure and traveling. I am good at creative problem solving and a good organizer and planner. I am stimulated by meeting people from cultures different from mine. I care about helping people improve their lives. Any ideas? It's a little difficult to network here. So I would appreciate any suggestions anyone has. I'm open.

I leave for Kenya August 22nd. We will spend about five days there before we go to Arusha in Tanzania. We might do a hot air balloon ride over a game park in Kenya first. In Arusha we will find a safari outfit and visit at least two game parks for four or five days. I will buy my ebony carvings in Arusha. Then we will go to Mt. Kilimanjaro, not to climb but to raise a gin and tonic to the memory of Ernest Hemingway and F. Scott Fitzgerald from some comfortable spot at the base. Decadent I remain. Then we fly to Da es Salaam from where we will get a hydrofoil to go to Zanzibar for a few days. We return to Da al Salaam on the 9th of September and fly to Addis Abba on the 10th. We will stay one night in Ethiopia before returning to Sana'a the afternoon of the 11th. So that's all for now folks. I hope all is well with all of you.

Until Next Time.

A boy with his goats

A girl in the suq

A proud boy

September 21, 1993

Hi Everyone,

I'm back from my three week trip to East Africa, tired and very glad to crawl between the sheets of my mattress on the floor. It's my home. Funny what almost two years of living in the Developing World will do to your expectations of material comfort. As long as I have electricity, running water, a hot shower, and a way to boil water and cook a simple meal, I can deal.

My first impression of Nairobi was wow! It is a huge modern city with skyscrapers, paved streets, and abundant services. We (Muriel, Gladys and I) stayed in the Parkside Hotel near the Peace Corps office which offers a special deal to PCVs. We had a triple for $5 a night apiece. It was a real bargain, clean, bathroom, good towels and nice location. Its restaurant is frequented by volunteers as the food prices are reasonable and the menu agrees with American tastes. Beer flows in great quantities! Every morning I ate eggs and BACON for breakfast, to hell with the cholesterol! In fact I think I ate more bacon those three weeks in East Africa than I have in the last ten years all together.

We enjoyed window shopping in modern department stores, checking out the ebony shops, and eating in a more than passable Italian restaurant where I enjoyed spaghetti carbonara and a good dry red wine.

Gladys, Muriel and me at the Karen Blixen house

We took a couple of excursions outside the city. We went to Bombas where we saw tribal groups perform their dances. Quite good but very much set up for tourists. More delightful was our visit to the Karen Blixen's (Isak Dinesen) house of OUT OF AFRICA fame. What a lovely setting and house although the inside was quite dark with mahogany wood in abundance. The inside of the house was not used for the movie we were told as it is too small. But the scenes of the outside and the setting are the same as the movie. The Ngong Hills where Denys is buried are visible from the back yard. I bought a copy of Dinesen's book on which the movie is based and enjoyed rereading it throughout our sojourn in Kenya and Tanzania.

In our discussions with the Kenya PCVs we learned of a nice hotel on the shores of Lake Victoria that offers Peace Corps Volunteers good rates. So we made the six hour bus trip to Kisumu and the Victorian era Hotel Royale complete with wicker furniture on the porch, ceiling fans and mosquito nets over each bed.

We went by taxi to a quaint restaurant on the lake for a pretty decent lunch near Hippo Point but didn't see any hippos as it was the middle of the day, and they don't come out of the water in the heat. The lake is very beautiful, and I was tempted to go for a swim which of course is impossible because the water is infected with the snail carrying bilharzia.

Fishermen on Lake Victoria

As malaria is prevalent in East Africa, we were on chloroquine which we started to take weekly in Yemen before out trip, and then, once in Kenya, we took two pills a day for the chloroquine resistant malaria. Although I was bitten by many mosquitoes on my journey and sometimes had to sleep under the mosquito net to escape the pesky creatures, I am without any sign of malaria. We had a tedious bus ride back to Nairobi so that we could go in a group taxi to the Tanzania border.

The countryside is beautiful, lush green and peopled with brightly clothed Africans. It was so good to see green, especially the hedge like tea fields being harvested when we were there. I was reminded of Hemingway's THE GREEN HILLS OF AFRICA which I want to reread when I get a chance.

It was so good to see women on the streets dressed in bright clothing that looked so good against their dark skin. It was especially good to see their faces and to see men and women talking together, walking together, and socializing with each other in restaurants. It was nice to go into restaurants and not be the only women in them. In fact, one of my greatest sensations was the sense of freedom. The Kenyans are warm people. They speak to you and welcome you. "Jumbo", welcome, we heard everywhere. We became aware of the restrictions and stress that life holds for us in Yemen which I guess I have come to accept as normal. The life of the PCVs in Kenya seems much easier because the society is more open and accepting. I couldn't stop reading signs in English. It was so great to understand what they said. Of course there are political problems in Kenya, and since we left we have heard that the problems are growing, but I liked Kenya very much. I saw it through different eyes coming from Yemen than I would see it coming directly from the States.

We traveled to the Tanzania border in a group taxi for about $2.50. The taxis are similar to the ones in Yemen although they seemed to be in better condition and the drivers not as crazy. But to be fair, we weren't climbing mountains and driving through mountain passes. In the taxi we talked with a young couple going to Arusha, too. He was from Tanzania, and she was British. They had met at college in London. He was very helpful walking us across the border and through customs. He also changed our remaining Kenya shillings into Tanzania shillings for us on the black market. We then got another group taxi to go to Arusha about two hours away.

Our main purpose for going to Arusha was to book a safari. After much reading and discussion with different agencies, we decided on a four day, three night safari with Amango. Because it was the end of winter in East Africa, and the nights were cold, we decided to stay in lodges. This decision, of course, jacked the price up. It cost us $525 apiece. But it included all food, our private land rover and driver/guide.

The first day, we drove to the Seronera Lodge in the Serengeti National Park. Along the way we had lunch at the lodge at Lake Manyara. All the lodges were comfortable and interesting. The food was okay but not exceptional. At Lobo Wildlife Lodge where we stayed the second night, I enjoyed having a drink in front of a roaring fire in the fire place.

Our guide and land rover

The second day we went on a daylong drive seeing many animals of all kinds. The same was true of the remaining days. I was most impressed seeing elephants in their natural habitat. I must say I cannot understand how anyone could ever get any pleasure shooting any of these animals, especially the elephants. The giraffes were just awesome. The lions seemed bored with the people there to see them. I felt like I was driving around in a cage while the animals stared at us.

The Serengeti is huge. We saw only a fraction of it. We kept running into Eric who was at the end of his six week trip in East Africa. He had left August 1st and spent a week in Ethiopia and a couple of weeks in Uganda. He also climbed Mt. Kilimanjaro. The game drives were long, dusty affairs. After a while they get a little tedious. We didn't go on a balloon ride as it was too costly, $275 for an hour.

Hippopotamuses enjoying a swim

Massai women

Massai hunter

Our last night we drove to Ngorongoro Crater and stayed in the crater lodge on the rim overlooking the crater. It was a spectacular view. On the way there we passed by the Olduvai Gorge where the Leakeys found the human fossil remains. We paused to see it in the distance, but didn't go up close. On our last day we drove to the floor of the crater. The big show was to see the rhinoceroses. Their numbers are being depleted, and a serious effort is being made to protect them from poachers who want their horns. Yemen imports the horns to make jambiya handles.

Back in Arusha we went ebony shopping and made arrangements to go to Moshi to see Mt Kilimanjaro. We stayed at the YWCA there. The clouds were really low, and we could not see the peak even though we drove around in our hired car and waited patiently for a day and a half. At the end of our trip on the way to Addas Abba in Ethiopia we stopped at the Kilimanjaro Airport. When we took off, the pilot flew close to the mountain, and we saw the spectacular top very clearly.

Gladys and Muriel at the base of Kilimanjaro

Mt. Kilimanjaro

We flew to Dar es Salaam for an overnight before we took the hydrofoil to Zanzibar. At the airport we met Eric again, and he joined us for the remainder of our trip.

The hydrofoil took a little over an hour. Zanzibar is magnificent. The old city is quaint and heavily Muslim but refreshingly colored by Africa. We toured the city, had a beer at the Africa House overlooking the Indian Ocean, and went on a spice tour. The tour took us to the old slave quarters where the slaves were detained, bought and sold before beginning their sad journey to the USA. It made me feel a little queasy when the guide talked about the US's role in the slave trade.

After two days in the old city we left for the undeveloped beaches on the east side of the island. Words fail me here. Miles of untouched beaches. Palm trees on the shore. The water was a bright green. Our little bungalow was on the shore, close to the water. But of course there are downsides to untouched paradises. There was no electricity. They brought us hurricane lamps each night. We had running water about two hours a day and you never knew when it would be running. When we could take showers it was salt water!

The big disappointment was that there was only one little restaurant run by the people who owned the bungalows. The food was horrible. The only fish we were served was a square piece of calamari which was so over cooked it was like trying to eat a Goodyear tire. As we had no cooking facilities in the house we had to eat out. We heard through the grapevine that we should try to make contact with one of the villagers who lived close by. They would cook dinner for tourists in their houses as long as the bungalow owners didn't know it. So Eric made contact with a small boy, and we were set to go for dinner at his house at 7 pm.

We bought a lobster from a fisherman which Eric delivered to the cook. We stumbled our way into the village by flashlight. Two French girls joined us for the meal. We were shown into a dark house and sat in a narrow hallway on the floor Yemeni style. Our knees touched each other. The food was brought in and placed on the floor. We had only one small candle to see and eat by. The rice was abundant, the octopus sauce and mixed vegetables meager. Our lobster was brought to us with nothing to crack it open or pick the meat out, so we couldn't get all the meat out of the shells. We were also served two coconuts unopened, making them impossible to eat. While we did the best we could eating our meal, the children in the family hovered in doorways watching us eat. We could only see their shadows, but they kept coughing on us as we ate. An adventure. But we have had a good time remembering this dinner.

Muriel, Gladys, and Eric in front of our bungalow

Reading in Paradise

After two days in paradise we returned to the city and went back to Dar es Salaam to catch our flight to Addas Abba the next morning at 6am. We arrived in Addas Abba about one pm, and the Ethiopian airlines helped us get transit visas so that we could go into town. They also took us to a decent hotel, put us up for the night and gave us lunch, dinner, and breakfast. Addas Abba seemed to be a modern city. But you must remember I'm seeing it through Yemeni eyes. We took a taxi to a church on the hills outside the city and saw massive poverty. It was haunting, encompassing a larger area than I've seen in Yemen. It was on the scale of what I saw in India in 1972. The area was lush green. Why is there so much poverty? September 11th we returned to Sana'a. It was a long, eventful trip. It made me realize that I am ready to go back home.

Back in Sana'a I am awaiting news about what I'll be teaching and when the University will start classes. No word yet. I'm also working on an APA proposal Anne and I wrote to build a structure to house the sewing machines donated by Japan for the Women's Center. We hope to get it approved during October and supervise the building of it in November. All's well. I hope all is going well with all of you.

So long for now.

House similar to the one where we had dinner

October 25, 1993

Hello Everyone,

I am still waiting for the University to begin classes this fall. Almost a month ago now we had a department meeting and learned what our teaching assignments will be. I'm to teach two classes of sophomore grammar and one class of sophomore reading. I began to gather materials and have text book photocopies (at my expense) as of course there are no books available that will meet my needs at the University. Thank goodness for the Peace Corps resource library and YALI (the Yemen American Institute) where three volunteers teach. They have a good resource library as well.

We learned the Friday before classes were to begin on October 2nd that the University wouldn't open because 30,000 freshmen candidates in Yemen had been denied admittance to the University in Sana'a or one of the branch colleges. The irate students denied admittance demonstrated daily in the streets near the University. As a result, the government ordered the university system to accept the students. Of course there is no room for them, nor the teachers, or money to pay the teachers they already have. By this action the government put the onus on the University and effectively washed their hands of the matter. The University didn't open as scheduled and is still doing battle with the Ministry of Education, trying to work out a compromise. We went to a meeting on Saturday to learn, we hoped, when classes would begin. Again we were put on hold and told to go home until the 30th of October.

Perhaps we will begin to administer entrance exams beginning the 30th to freshmen who want to study in the English Education Department to determine if their English fluency is good enough for them to be accepted by the department. Of course those students who fail the test have recourse if their families are powerful. Complaints will be made, and perhaps money will exchange hands. We are just waiting to see what decisions will be made. Probably now classes won't begin until the middle of November.

This uncertainty makes those of us who are supposed to leave the end of January nervous because we wonder when the semester will end. But I cannot imagine the semester being prolonged because Ramadan begins around the 12th of February. Surely the University administration will want the first semester done with, including exams, before that date. In all probability we will have a shortened semester of six to eight weeks. Wow! However this situation is resolved, it will be the teachers and the students who have to bear the brunt of political and administrative decisions. Our classes will be over loaded. So long to the sixty in a class rule. Various elements of society will complain, of course, about teachers and the poor quality of education students are receiving and how expensive it all is.

So we play bridge, read, wander around Sana'a, talk, and wait. I sit in my window and look at the street scene below. Painters with long handled rollers sit on the sidewalk waiting to be selected for painting jobs; peddlers push carts of tinware and household items, clothes, and buttagas; some peddlers have fashioned cases filled with sweets on the front of bicycles they peddle around the city in search of customers; a good humor man goes by with his cart; an occasional donkey pulls a cart; a herd of goats stops to eat at the overflowing dumpster before being pushed along by their herder; a cripple unable to stand crawls along the sidewalk on his hands and knees begging, "ana miskeen"; a woman walks by with a buttagas tank on her head; a young boy rolls a buttagas tank in the street, pushing it with his feet; men pass carrying chickens by their wings they'll kill for lunch; school children with book bags ring our door bells hoping to see the Americans; a sea of women all in black drift by. Who are they? How old are they? What do they think? Feel? They move silently, anonymously by my window. "Allah akba. Allah akba." Twelve o'clock; time to eat lunch.

A typical street scene in Sana'a

Last week Muriel and I went to Sa'da in the north of Yemen near the Saudi Arabia border. Sa'da is an ancient walled city and one of the most conservative tribal areas in Yemen. We arrived in the dusty brown place after a long five hour bus ride. We went immediately in search of the Mareb Hotel mentioned in the *Lonely Planet*. It was a terrible one sheet, dirty place with a shared bathroom. We rested for an hour to avoid the intense sun before we went out to explore the city. We walked on top of the wall around the city. It was amazing. The wall is twenty feet high in places, and the walkway must be at least ten feet wide. The guide book says it was built wide enough so that a donkey with a cart could easily trot along. In places the wall has tumbled down, and you have to step down to street level. In other places the wall has been breached to make it possible for cars to enter the city. Over all it is in remarkably good shape. As we strolled around the wall, looking down into narrow alleys, gardens, private courtyards, five story houses trimmed with alabaster and then out into the vast empty plain, I imagined that this must be what the wall around Troy must have looked like as Hector squinted into the midafternoon sun watching the approach of the Greek army.

Muriel and I on the wall surrounding Sa'da

After we left the wall we wandered in the streets of Sa'da, visiting some of the Jewish silver shops. They look and dress just like other Yemenis. Only the lock of hair identifies them as Jewish. We drank tea in an outside garden that we felt comfortable in because there was another woman there, a German tourist.

After chicken and rice at a local restaurant we started back to the Mareb Hotel which neither of us wanted to return to. So we decided to look for another hotel we had heard about. It was much cleaner, safer and had two clean sheets on the beds! We went back to our hotel, got our luggage and left. We were out 200 riyals (two dollars apiece) for the old hotel, but it was worth it. The new hotel cost us each 400 riyals.

On the way back to Sana'a the next morning in a group taxi, we met a young British chap who had just come to Yemen to study the baboon population said to exist here (I've never seen any). He told us he was interested in studying them because unlike baboons in the rest of the world, the ones found in Yemen, Saudi Arabia, Somalia and Sudan live in patriarchal societies, not matriarchal ones. I'M NOT SURPRISED!! Anyway, we have since met him for tea, and I expect we'll see him again.

Last week at the American Women's Group meeting I ran into a Palestinian woman I know who markets handmade Palestinian articles, featuring their famous cross stitch. As I am an admirer of their work, I asked her when I could visit her at her house where she sells the items. That afternoon Muriel and I entered the Palestinian compound where many of the refugees live. Her husband, an old PLO soldier who is not well because of past battles and wounds, met us at the gate in his car to take us to their house. Most of the houses in the compound are simple. The PLO flag is everywhere. 'Umm Bakr (meaning the mother of Bakr) served us tea and displayed her beautiful bags, scarves, sweaters, and pants. They are expensive as she sells mainly to rich ex-pat women. Although I would have loved one of everything, I only could afford to buy a couple of items.

A photograph of Arafat nestled between crossed PLO flags stared down from the wall at us. 'Umm Bakr showed us a needlepoint book that Arafat had autographed for her. Her handsome sons, one of them Bakr, came to meet us. The other son was one of Muriel's students at the University. He was excited to see her in his home.

'Umm Bakr told us that she was praying for peace. She hopes that peace with Israel happens because there has been enough death. She had to leave Palestine in the late 1940's and has been a refugee ever since. First she lived in Lebanon until their civil war. Then she moved to Jordan and, finally, Yemen. She has supported her family as well as helped other Palestinian women by marketing their hand made articles.

Our department chair at the University just called to ask if we would come to the University this afternoon to help him collate the freshmen exams. Maybe there is hope because he said we will begin to administer tests on Saturday and will begin classes on Sunday, October 31st. Things may change, but it looks hopeful at the moment.

(October 29, 1993)

The eight of us left in my group who came to Yemen in November, 1991, just finished a three-day COS (close of service) conference at the Peace Corps office. They gave us information about what services the Returned Peace Corps Office in Washington will offer us and told us what the procedure is for ending our tour here. We also had some touchy feely sessions about feeling proud of ourselves, and advice and a game plan for reentry and adjusting to the Western World again. Flush toilet paper down the toilet; eat with silverware; don't use bread as a utensil to stick into the serving dish; the left hand is clean and worthy of respect; skirts don't have to be ankle length; upper arms are not sexual objects; sit in chairs, not crossed legged on the floor, and of course much, much more. We talked about the broader aspects of reentry as well. So much has happened at home while we have been on another planet, both in the society and to the people we know and care about. Reentry, we were warned, in not easy, and we should be prepared for experiencing cultural shock.

I am looking forward to catching up on new gadgets, TV programs, movies, music, books, and clothes. I can't wait to drive a car again. It's hard to concentrate on starting school because I'm thinking about home. I don't want to arrive in New Hampshire in February!! I'd freeze to death after the wonderful weather here. So, at the moment, I'm planning to fly to Amman and travel around Jordan, slip in and out of Israel, and then drive through Syria on a bus, stopping at a few places. I plan to fly to Turkey for several days, fly to Italy from Istanbul. I'd like to spend most of my Italian time in Sicily and Venice. Finally Paris for a few days visiting old haunts before I return to the States. Of course all this might change, but I'll probably arrive in Boston sometime in March.

Our SPA project was approved so Anne and I will begin the supervision of a $10,000 building at the Women's Training Center. I'm very excited about that as I feel close to the Center. I feel good about my work there. The story I wrote for the UN project to make Yemeni children more sensitive to the refugees from Somalia has been translated into Arabic. But that project seems bogged down at the moment. I don't know where it's going. Last night I went to a big Halloween party at the home of one of the women in the American Women's Group I know. It was good fun. Open bar and dancing in the courtyard.
So that's all for now folks.

I hope all is well with all of you,

November 20, 1993

Greetings Everyone,

I hope this letter reaches you before Thanksgiving, but it probably won't because the mail will probably be clogged with cards and greetings from people States side. It doesn't seem possible that this will be the third holiday season away from the USA. Time has gone so fast. Anyway, one of the volunteers is being medevac'd to Washington tonight so I asked her to mail this letter for me.

I started my fourth week at the University today. So far things are going well. I am really enjoying my classes. The students I'm teaching are studying to be English teachers so their English is quite good. They can understand what I'm saying. There is a problem getting materials and running off tests and quizzes. For instance, I'm going to give my two grammar classes a quiz on Tuesday. I had the 120 one-page quizzes run off at a riyal apiece (about $2.50 total). When I hand out the quizzes I'll have to collect one and a half riyals from each of them. Can you imagine? I know you are probably thinking I should pay for the quiz myself. But $2.50 is a significant amount of money here. Right now the dollar is worth almost 60 riyals. Inflation is rampant. The students accept this way of doing things as normal.

One of my big classroom behavior modification projects is to get students not to throw paper on the floor. They are so used to dropping anything they don't want on the floor: paper, paper tea cups, cigarette butts. They observe me picking the refuge up and still they drop stuff anyway (not to watch me work because they are not like American students this way). It's just the cultural norm. All Yemenis drop things they don't want in the streets and in public buildings. I keep a bag in the room for them to dump their stuff in and don't allow smoking in my room. Today my room was especially messy so I hired the cleaning lady who was sweeping the hallway to sweep for me. The cleaning staff never clean the rooms, just the hallways. Some of my students saw me give her money and were embarrassed that I did that. I hope they will be more conscious of keeping the room clean. At any rate, it is the cleanest room in the area. The building is fairly new, but it is a mess. For some reason there is no running water in it so all the bathrooms are locked up.

The other day I had lunch with Muhammad Jafah and his friend in the new student cafeteria near my building. It is nice, fairly clean, and the food reasonably good. I was the only woman eating there. I went into the restroom to wash my hands. It was crowded with women students eating lunch in there in what I would call an unpleasant situation. Of course they couldn't unveil and eat in front of men. So they ate in the bathroom. There was a whole bank of modern sinks in the bathroom, but no water. I had to go into one of the stalls and turn on the little faucet next to the Turkish toilet in order to get water to wash my hands.

A qat chew at my house. From the left: Muhammad Jafah, Muhammad Mokbel, Yassine, Dr Shama (the Indian professor), me, Khalid

Khalid teaching Eric how to dance Yemeni style

Resting and chewing qat

There is a great fish market about a half mile from where I live that has fresh fish delivered daily from Al-Hudayda. Now that the weather is cooler I buy fish there fairly regularly. Yesterday I bought a kilo of tuna. The salesman cut the filets right off the fish as I stood there. The fish cost 50 riyals (under a dollar). I marinated the filets in olive oil and spices and then fried them. The tuna was delicious. Last week I bought a half kilo of prawns for 130 riyals (a little under $2.50) and stir fried them with vegetables. Fresh fish is abundant and inexpensive. I'm going to try to cook red snapper soon. So, ironically, I can afford to buy and prepare good fish in Yemen that I would find cost prohibitive at home. In fact Thanksgiving morning some of us are going to have a feast of shrimp cocktails with Bloody Marys. We can't find a turkey, but we can eat great shrimp.

The political situation is heated here, caused by the on-going friction between the North and the South. Rumors abound. I'm so used to the rumors that I no longer pay much attention to them. I do know that inflation is high and Yemenis are upset. We wonder if there will be more food riots as there were a year ago. The banks don't have any dollars which is probably why the dollar is now worth so much on the black market. I wish I had some dollars to float on the market, but I spent all mine in Africa, putting me in the same boat as the Yemenis. OK, well, that's what the Peace Corps experience is all about.

Stay well and have a nice Thanksgiving,

January 2, 1994

Happy New Year Everyone!

I know, I know. It's been a long time since I've written. My intentions were the best, but I just didn't get to it. I'll now attempt to bring you up to date with what's happening in my life since my last letter written before Thanksgiving.

Thanksgiving Day was full of food and dishes to wash. But at least our pots, pans and dishes are few! I did a brunch for the PC volunteers in Sana'a for the holiday. The center of the meal was shrimp and homemade cocktail sauce. I was lucky to find some horseradish to give the proper zing to the sauce and to the Bloody Marys (Vodka given to us by a sympathetic ex-pat).

In the middle of the afternoon Muriel and I went to the Embassy nurse's home for the real feast. Most of the other volunteers went to the Embassy for the traditional meal. BJ and her husband feel a special affinity for Muriel and me because we went through the Rose-broken-leg experience with her after we arrived back in Sana'a with the wounded Rose a year ago. She called and invited us to have dinner with them at the Pipe Line Restaurant, a special restaurant for the Hunt Oil Company employees. Ken works for Hunt Oil. The food is American, served cafeteria style. On Thanksgiving Day, turkey and the fixings were served.

Eric, his girlfriend Karen (a new volunteer), and Maryanne (a nurse volunteer from my group of PCV's who stays with us when she is in town) were with us for the holiday so we had a full house. Our guests camped out on the mafraj cushions.

The morning after Thanksgiving Cecilia Hitte, our PC director, arrived bright and early to inform us that Mahonney, the director of the Yemen American Language Institute where three volunteers in my group teach, had been kidnapped the evening before and that we were not to leave the building except to go to a dukan for food until further notice because it wasn't known if this was a terrorist act or a tribal issue. To draw attention to their demands and to get government action tribes often kidnap foreigners. According to reports, if Mahonney's capture was a tribal issue, he would be well treated, given good food, qat and souvenirs. As he speaks excellent Arabic he would be able to converse with his captors. His capture hit a little too close to home as he was captured in front of a Western grocery store where I periodically shop. Understandably, things were tense in the American community for the week of his captivity. Late that night we were given the all clear to move about as usual as the Embassy had established that the kidnapping was a tribal issue.

One unsubstantiated rumor is that he is a CIA agent and that is why the US government was willing to pay the one million they supposedly did for his release. I don't know if any of this is true, but the diplomatic staff is supposedly crawling with CIA agents. Don't ask me why. I can't imagine that Yemen endangers US security. For me it is disillusioning to think that the CIA has infiltrated the cultural and educational agencies abroad, and I hope none of the above CIA connection rumors are true. I personally resent the suspicion of many Yemenis, including my friend Yassin, that Peace Corps Volunteers are CIA agents. What an insult!!

Our money for the Women Center's building to house the sewing machines given by Japan has arrived, and construction is underway. Anne and I hope that everything can be finished before we leave Yemen. We have arranged with Michael, a volunteer who is not going to COS when we do, to oversee the project until it is completed, if necessary. At any rate I am proud of this project.

Exterior of our building at the Women's Center

Interior of the building

Michael with the basket weavers

The stories about the Somali refugees for Yemeni school children that I helped write are almost finished, but they will not be completely finished before I leave Yemen. The committee has told me that they will send me a copy of the printed books.

Christmas week abounded with parties. I went to the annual Embassy party given by the Ambassador and his wife. Good food and music. The party gave me an opportunity to say good-bye to some of the ex-pat women I have come to know in the American Women's Group. I also worked on the American Women's bazaar to raise money for charity. A lot of the money will go to the Women's Center. Therefore, I have a vested interest in the funds raised.

Anne and her boyfriend hosted a great party for us and some of their ex-pat friends at the house where I house sat last summer.

Anne and Rob

Christmas Day was filled with goodies. I did another brunch. Then a group of us went to the Sheraton Chinese restaurant for lunch and back to BJ's that night at the Pipe Line Restaurant. Our new PCMO (medical officer) Kim and her husband joined us. Kim and Greg are big bridge players so they invited June, Muriel and me to their house New Year's Eve for bridge and great pizza Kim made, the best pizza I've had since I left the States.

Classes at the University are still limping along. We don't know when the semester will officially finish. But I'm bringing mine to a close this week and will be available for students who need help next week. I have a lot of things to take care of before I leave January 31st.

Remember my writing about Christine, the TWA employee from Boston whom we met in Egypt a year ago? Recently we heard from her, and she is planning to come to Sana'a for a five-day visit January 11th. I'm so excited about the prospect of showing Sana'a to someone from home. It will also give me a good opportunity to make my final tours around the Old City and other places I love in Sana'a. I'm going to arrange a qat chew in her honor. She has told me that she will take a suitcase back to Boston with her which I'll pick up from her when I return to the States. That will be a great savings for me. I just hope she can get off the ground as she will be flying space available.

The adventure is almost over. I already have my plane ticket that includes stops in Amman, Jordan, Istanbul, Rome, Paris, and Amsterdam. I plan to travel around the cities by public buses and go to Syria and Israel. I'll have to get a visa in Jordan to travel over the King Hussein Bridge into the occupied West Bank to travel in Israel. As Jordan and Israel have no travel agreements or treaty between them, this is the only way to go from Jordan to Israel and return to Jordan. I have to make sure Israeli custom officers don't stamp my passport. If they do I won't be allowed back in Jordan.

Muriel is going to travel with me as far as Istanbul and then return to Yemen, and I'll continue on by myself to Europe with stops in Rome, Florence, Sienna and Venice. Then I'll take a train to Paris and spend a few days sitting in cafes and touring the refurbished Louvre. Finally, I'll fly to Amsterdam for a couple of days before I fly home. Roughly, I plan to spend three to four weeks traveling with Muriel and two to three weeks traveling by myself in Europe. Money, good times, and weather will be the determining factors. I'm dreading the cold, and I don't have appropriate clothing with me for cold weather. I should be Stateside by the middle of March if not before, but don't look for me until you see the whites of my eyes. At any rate, I'll probably arrive in Boston before Easter.

Muriel with her students

Eric, Muriel, and Artis

I'm getting excited about traveling and going home, but I'm also sad about leaving Yemen. It's going to be difficult to say good-bye to my Yemeni friends. The American Peace Corps friends I can see Stateside, but I probably won't ever come back to Yemen, and most of my Yemeni friends will never travel to the States. I really hope that at least Khalid will visit me some day. It is going to be very difficult to say good-bye to him. The next three weeks will be emotionally draining with good-bye qat chews and my last views of Sana'a.

These last two years have been a great adventure, and I've learned so much. Yemen will always be a special place to me. The Peace Corps experience is not an easy one. The working life requires much patience and understanding. The status of women is difficult to accept. But certainly a new world was opened to me. I have met people from most countries in the Arab World. While the governments of Iraq and the USA rattled their sabers, I made friends with Iraqis and taught Iraqi students. While the World watches the Middle East peace talks presently underway and wonders what the results will be, I have befriended Palestinian refugees. I'm not yet sure how my political views have changed. Only reentry and time at home will demonstrate my changes in attitude. One thing is for certain, I will never be able to make blanket assumptions about all Arabs again. For all the political upheaval in Yemen, I'm safer walking the streets of Sana'a by myself at night than I would feel in Boston by myself at night. That says something. The future of Yemen is uncertain. But it was a rare privilege to live in an ancient culture trying to come to terms with the 20th Century and democracy.

On the 30th anniversary of Kennedy's assassination in November my reading class was holding a panel discussion on a story that was in the YEMEN TIMES. It was titled "The Whole World is Waiting". The main idea of the article was that while the two Ali's (North and South leaders) carry out their battle between each other, the Yemeni people are being crippled by high inflation, no jobs, as well as fear of civil war. My students come from all over Yemen, North and South. The main focus of their discussion was democracy. The consensus of opinion was that there is no democracy in Yemen. They criticized both Ali's, the government and the USA. They kept looking at me when they criticized the USA. I said nothing until the discussion ended. Then I told them how proud I was of them for conducting such an open ended, organized discussion in English and that they were participating in the democratic spirit of free speech. If there were no democracy in Yemen, I reminded them, such a discussion would never have taken place. Then I told them about President Kennedy and his call to my generation, "Ask not what your country can do for you. Ask what you can do for your country." Perhaps they should ask themselves the same question, I told them. That hour in the classroom will always remain one of my finest hours, and that famous line now has added meaning for me as does the word democracy. I think President Kennedy would have approved of the discussion.

In spite of the homesickness, dust, filth, lack of conveniences, political unrest, and the unenlightened attitude toward women, I wouldn't have given up a moment of the experience. I feel a warm sense of accomplishment because I fulfilled my two year commitment and was one of eight survivors in my original group of sixteen. I leave Yemen having learned and gained more than I leave behind. I wish you all could have such a life changing experience.

I thank all of you for your letters, phone calls, care packages, and money and clothes for me and the Women's Center. Your thoughtfulness and encouragement will always be remembered. So ends my letters from Yemen.

Until we meet again stateside,

Yours truly with a pal

The Old City of Sana'a, Yemen

Afterword

Early on the morning of January 31, 1994, Muhammad Jahaf, Muhammad Mokbel and Yassin Al-Hemeary picked up Muriel and me in a car they had borrowed from a friend to drive us to the airport to catch a flight to Amman, Jordan. Khalid Al-Yabari had come by our apartment building the night before to say good-bye. To say that saying good-bye to these friends was difficult is an understatement. They waited with us in the airport for our flight to be announced. I wanted so much to hug them each, but that would have caused them great embarrassment because a show of such affection in public is not done, especially hugging between a woman and a man. So I shook hands with them and left Yemen probably forever.

Amman became our focal point from which Muriel and I traveled down the Jordan Valley to Petra, the hidden city of the Nabateans. To reach the city we had to travel along a narrow pathway on donkeys. We arrived in a spectacular ancient ruin with amazing buildings carved into rock. Petra was an important city on the incense route that camels laden with frankincense and myrrh took north to Egypt and countries of the Roman Empire. This ancient route existed between the 11th Century BC and the 4th Century AD. We also went into Israel from Jordan and spent several days exploring the country. We stayed in Jerusalem in the Arab quarter near the Damascus Gate. When we returned to Jordan we went by bus into Syria and north to Damascus. I particularly found Damascus fascinating and decided I would like to live there for a while in the future. That future will never come.

After our stop in Amman, we flew to Istanbul where we found it very cold. We were used to warmer weather in Yemen and didn't have appropriate clothing to keep us warm. It also rained a lot when we were there, filling the streets with cold water. I discovered that my tennis shoes that I had worn for two years had developed some holes. Wet feet also contributed to my discomfort. We liked Istanbul, visited the famous sites tourists go to, enjoyed a Turkish bath and Turkish food, but the cold weather was overwhelming for us. Therefore, we decided to end our trip earlier than planned. Muriel flew back to Yemen, and I flew to the USA, skipping my planned visit to Europe. I arrived back in cold New Hampshire the end of February. But at least I could unpack some warm clothes I had stored at my brother's house, and my brother and sister-in-law kindly let me stay with them until I could find myself.

I remember reading a quote from a Returned Peace Corps Volunteer (RPCV) before I went to Yemen. The volunteer had written that the hardest thing about Peace Corps was coming home. That became my experience. I was truly a fish out of water. Grocery stores overwhelmed me with all the choices. Everything seemed to shine with cleanliness to the point of being startling. Everyone I knew was always in a hurry and didn't have time to sit and talk with me as my Yemeni friends did. My friends and family had gone on with their own lives, understandably, and most of them had only a passing interest in my experiences in Yemen. When civil war broke out in Yemen that May one friend said, "It's so fortunate you are not in Yemen anymore." I didn't think so. I wanted to be in Sana'a with my friends even though the city was being bombed. I stayed glued to CNN following the developments in the country. When the volunteers were flown out of Yemen to Washington, DC, I went there to meet them. The truth was, I was disoriented and wanted to go back to Yemen where my life was. I came to realize that my reentry experience was normal because most RPCV's have similar experiences adjusting to life in the States again.

Yemen's problems continue. After decades, Ali Abdullah Salah was removed from the presidency. He was in essence a dictator. Unemployment and tribal infighting continue. The revolt during the Arab Spring resulted in many deaths and loss of property. Instability remains a problem for this struggling country. Al-Qaeda has established a stronghold in Yemen. They became widely known as a terrorist group in the mid to late 1990's. The Cole, an American naval ship, was bombed near Aden. Dr. Martha, the doctor I wrote about on my trip to Ibb to visit Eric, was assassinated in the Baptist hospital operating room in Jibla. A British tour group was kidnapped and held hostage in a remote area of South Yemen. Some of the tourists were killed, and others were wounded, thus ending the romantic notion of what being kidnapped in Yemen was like. The drone attacks must add worry and fear to the lives of the average Yemeni. I can just imagine the negative reaction to the attacks of my Yemeni friends.

I lost contact with my friends in Yemen during the Iraq War, beginning in 2003. I think of them often and wonder what their lives are like. The young men who befriended me are in their 40's now. Elham's sons have grown up and are probably married and have families of their own. I wonder if she is still teaching English.

I moved to El Paso and feel at home here. The weather and topography remind me of Sana'a. I love the cultural mix of El Paso, the Mexican customs, food, and the friendliness of people in the Southwest. Although I adjusted to life back in the States again in a few months' time, I think of Yemen often, missing it, my friends, and the life I had there twenty years ago. Being a Peace Corps Volunteer in Yemen was a life changing experience. I know my views of the Arab World are very different from what they were before I lived there. Part of me didn't come home. Yemen for all its problems will always be close to my heart.

El Paso, November 6, 2013

APPENDIX

Certificate of Appreciation

is presented to

Mary Lou Currier

In recognition of dedicated service
and outstanding contributions toward
sustainable development, global
understanding, and world peace
while serving as a
Peace Corps Volunteer in

Yemen

Director, Peace Corps

President of the United States

U.S. PEACE CORPS

Sana'a - Republic of Yemen

P.O. Box: 1151

Phone : 73326, 275504

Fax : 275503

هيئة السلام للولايات المتحده الامريكيه

صنعاء . الجمهوريه اليمنيه

ص . ب : ١١٥١

تلفون : ٢٧٥٥٠٤ , ٧٣٣٢٦

فـاكس : ٢٧٥٥٠٣

DESCRIPTION OF SERVICE
MARY LOU CURRIER SSN 003-30-4698
Republic of Yemen November 1991 - January 1994

Mary Lou Currier began twelve weeks of pre-service training in Sana, Yemen, November 10, 1991. This intensive training consisted of the following courses of study: Arabic language, 220 classroom hours; cross cultural awareness, 60 classroom hours; personal health in the third world, 20 classroom hours; Teaching English as a Foreign Language (TEFL), 100 classroom hours.

The total hours spent in training, 400 classroom hours.

On January 31, 1992, Ms Currier was sworn in as a Peace Corps Volunteer and began her service as a teacher for the Ministry of Education in Yemen in the Faculty of Arts on the old campus at Sana'a University.

The following academic year (1992 -1993) she was assigned to the Faculty of Arts Education on the new campus of Sana'a University where she taught basic English to freshmen students preparing to be teachers.

In the fall of 1993 Ms Currier became a member of the Faculty of English Education where she taught reading and grammar to sophomore prospective English teachers.

During her time as a volunteer in Yemen, Ms Currier was involved with the following projects:

Women's Training Center

She was a volunteer in the Mother Child Care Unit at the Women's Training Center, established by the Social Organization for Family Development (SOFD) for the poor women and their families in the Asr area of Sana'a. Many of these families were forced to return to Yemen as a result of the Gulf War. These women are offered basic literacy classes, sewing and basket weaving classes, health and nutrition and instruction in caring for children. Ms Currier was also active in helping the Center market their products at local Western bazaars.

Somali Refugee Problem

She was a member of the Year of the Family Committee in conjunction with the United Nations High Commission for Refugees (UNHCR). The committee assumed the task of helping to raise the awareness on the part of Yemeni children concerning the unfortunate lives of the Somali refugees living in Yemen in response to the UN declaration making 1994 "The Year of the Family". The main project of the committee was to write stories for the school children in Yemen about the lives of refugees. Ms Currier participated in the writing of all three stories produced, writing one of the stories herself.

SPA Project for Clothing Factory

Ms Currier and another Peace Corps Volunteer wrote a Small Projects Assistance Proposal (SPA) to build a factory building at the Women's Training Center to house sewing equipment purchased by the Japaneese Government as a form of income generation for the poor women and for the Center. The proposal was approved, and $10,000 was allocated for the volunteers who oversaw the construction of the building with their Yemeni counterparts.

American Women's Group of Sana'a

She was a member of the Community Service Committee of the American Women's Group. The community service committee awarded funds to charitable organizations in Yemen. Ms Currier was particularly active on the education committee that awarded scholarships to deserving Yemeni women and purchased uniforms for the poor school children whose mothers attended the Women's Training Center. She also worked at the charity bazaars.

Women in Development Committee (WID)

She was an active member of the Peace Corps WID committee, helping to find secondary projects for other volunteers. As a member of the committee she was responsible for setting up a panel discussion in conjunction with the American Women's Group. The topic was "Educated Women in a Traditional Islamic Society". She also assisted in choosing the panel of Yemeni Women who participated in the discussion.

Workshops

Ms Currier attended workshops dealing with the following topics: Designing English curriculum around health issues in Yemen, Grant writing for SPA projects, and First Aid.

Pursuant to section 5(f) of the Peace Corps Act, 22U.S.C. and 2504(f), as amended, any former volunteer employed by the United States Government following Peace Corps Volunteer Service is entitled to have any period of satisfactory Peace Corps Volunteer service credited for purposes of retirement, seniority, reduction in force, leave and other privileges based on length of Government service.

This is to certify in accordance with Executive Order 11103 of April 10,1963, that Mary Lou Currier served satisfactorily as a Peace Corps Volunteer. Her service ended on January 31, 1994. Her benefits under the Executive Order extend for a period of one year after termination of volunteer service, except that the employing agency may extend the period for up to three years for a former volunteer who enters military service or pursues studies at a recognized institution of higher learning or engages in other activities which in the view of the appointing authority warrants extension of the period.

Ms Currier requests a Privacy Act Waiver, thereby providing for the release of a copy of her Description of Volunteer Service Statement to prospective employers, training organizations, academic institutions and other authorized agencies.

Mary Lou Currier 01/23/94

Mary Lou Currier   Date
Peace Corps Volunteer
Republic of Yemen

Cecelia Hilte 01/23/94

Cecelia Hilte   Date
Peace Corps Country
Director, Republic of
Yemen

Made in the USA
San Bernardino, CA
25 November 2015